A CHRISTIAN HISTORY OF

GOD'S HUMANS

FROM ADAM TO TODAY

By **Howard Ray White**,

Long Retired Professional Engineer,
Southern Historian and
Author of 22 Published Books.

Published by SouthernBooks in 2024.

ISBN #979-8-9877990-6-2

*A Christian History of God's Humans from Adam to
Today* is published by
SouthernBooks, Charlotte, North Carolina.

Dedication

I, Howard Ray White, dedicate this book to the millions of Americans who want to get to know Jesus but are hesitant and confused by the popularized and often school-taught notion that Christianity and the holy Bible are non-sense because we humans have simply evolved from primates like ancestors of human-like animals (**Homo Erectus** and **Homo Neanderthalensis**, etc.) and long-ago apes, chimpanzees and monkeys.

Do you want to learn the true history of our planet Earth, its living plants and animals and Adam and Eve?

Do you want to learn the history of mankind over the 10,000 generations that followed Adam and Eve?

Let's do it.

Please open this door and just walk in!

Howard Ray White

The Author, an 86-year-old Retired Chemical Engineer and Devout Christian, Explains.

It seems so hard today, and during my lifetime, for Americans and people of other nations to reconcile the two primary stories of the universe and humankind history.

1. The first story, seen in the Holy Bible, teaches us:

A. That God's creation of the Universe and, later, we humans, beginning with His creation of **Adam and Eve**, <u>occurred relatively recently in Earth's history, long after the last Ice Age.</u>

B. That, later, <u>a horrific Great Flood covered the Earth</u> and killed all humans, animals and birds except for Noah, his family and the animals and birds they saved in the huge boat they had built, the **Ark**.

2. The second story, presented to us through scientific and geographic research, especially in my 86-year lifetime, teaches us a greatly different story of the universe and humankind history:

A. Astronomers today reveal that the universe began by expanding in a "**Big Bang**" that occurred **13.9 billion years ago**, that the universe is huge, containing 200 billion trillion stars and that one of them, <u>our **Sun**, started to shine **4.6 billion years ago**</u>.

B. Scientific research in earth's rocks indicate that primitive life began on earth 0.9 billion years later, that being **3.7 billion years ago**.

4

C. The animals and the one that most resembles we humans, now deceased **Homo Erectus** and **Homo Neanderthalensis**, began life on earth, in Africa, about **2 million years ago**. There is evidence that they spread across Europe and Asia, but no evidence of any of them living beyond 40,000 years ago, during the last ice age, which concluded about 15,000 years ago.

D. There is scientific evidence that the **first humans** (homo sapiens) arrived on earth, in East Africa, about **200,000 years ago**.

E. There is scientific and geographic evidence that the huge flood that **Noah** encountered occurred at today's **Black Sea about 7,600 years ago**. There is no scientific evidence that this flood of Black Lake destroyed the lives of all animals, birds and destroyed all humans except for Noah's family.

Furthermore, it seems so hard today for young Americans to believe the Biblical history of mankind because, in American grammar schools, middle schools, colleges and universities, far too many teachers and professors discourage embracing Christianity, arguing than we humans simply evolved from earlier creatures that resembled us like **Homo Erectus** and **Homo Neanderthalensis (the Neanderthals)** or from **chimpanzees, monkeys or apes.**

So, if you are an elderly Christian struggling over your children's and/or grandchildren's skepticism

concerning Jesus, use this book, my book, to advantage.

So, if you, yourself, are struggling over the "we came from monkeys, idea," turn to this book, my book, <u>to gain insight that is helpful in recognizing that God is real, Christ is real and you need to accept them in your personal life</u>.

The major basis for understanding why the Bible and today's science do not fully agree is this:

God did not teach geography and science to his people. He enabled us, from Adam and Eve going forward over 10,000 generations, to discover so, so much, to work together, to learn from and teach others and advance human civilization. <u>And, goodness, our ancestors have learned a tremendous amount and humans today are still learning and, through acquired rapid food production, manufacturing and distribution methods, produced, delivered and remade our world</u>.

And this is the **Good News**:

The idea of God's creation of Mankind, as revealed in Genesis, and the idea of today's science and knowledge of Earth's history, do not have to disagree, if those concepts are intelligently understood.

There is more **Good News**:

Since God created mankind, we humans have, over a span of 10,000 generations, evolved into the diversified peoples who inhabit the Earth today.

6

A Brief Overview.

I will present information about human creation (Adam and Eve) and our subsequent evolution, based on the Holy Bible and today's scientific knowledge, to encourage you to think in terms of the **big picture**:

I will first cover the creation of the Universe and Earth.

Then, I will cover the creation of life.

Then, I will cover God's creation of man in east Africa, his population growth and a portion of man's eventual migration out of Africa and into the various continents of earth.

Then, I will explain how, trapped and isolated by Ice Age weather, humankind's "out of Africa" portion subsequently evolved into a very diverse population, thereby creating the four major races of man:

The African race,

The European race,

The Asian race

And the North and South America race.

Then, I will follow God's relationship with man through what I have defined as His seven Covenants, ending in the Covenant under which we live today, presented by His Son, Jesus Christ.

Then, I will explore the three major differentiating characteristics of man, which differ slightly among individuals (even among siblings) and slightly, but noticeably, among the races.

First, I should tell you that I am a Christian man. <u>I believe that God created the Universe and the Earth and the life that lives upon it.</u> I believe that God carried out that creation by employing the cosmic forces and evolutionary life forces that are observed by scientists today.

But, I believe, <u>God intervened supernaturally to create man in his own image – man did not evolve from animals merely through natural evolution.</u>

And, from that basis, I will proceed.

All people today are descended from God's creation of Adam and Eve, a supernatural event. We are not just highly evolved animals.

Unlike animals, each person has the gift of a soul that is capable of living an eternal life in the presence of God. And, through his son, Jesus Christ, God has revealed today's path to Heaven:

> *"For God so loved the world that He gave His one and only Son, that whoever believes in Him shall not perish, but have everlasting life."*

Contents

Introduction

Understanding how the concept of Creation and the concept of Evolution relate — one to the other — seems to become more and more perplexing throughout the world as each decade comes and goes. I was born in 1938. My goodness, just consider the advances in science that I have witnessed over the intervening 86 years, especially in human knowledge of the physical sciences and biology. What about the advances in human knowledge over the 200 years since my great, great grandfather was born?

How does, **Present Human Knowledge** compare to **Biblical Human Knowledge**?

For over 2,000 years God's revelations, through His prophets, have stood like a rock — not changing. On the other hand, over that span of over 20 centuries, human scientific knowledge has grown exponentially by leaps and bounds. So, can we students of *A Christian History of God's Humans from Adam to Today* make sense of the apparent ever-widening disagreement between these two foundations of human knowledge — foundations upon which human civilization and Christian faithfulness are continuing to be built?

Yes, that was my dilemma when I began to seriously study the issue twenty years ago. Following considerable personal research and study, I take comfort in finding a pathway that makes sense of the history of God's Humans.

I have found a pathway whereby apparent conflicts between:

1) the 4,000-to-6,000-year Biblical human teaching and

2) today's science-based human teaching

are resolved and seem to fade away.

The pathway to the understanding we humans seek is revealed, to a considerable extent, by our realizing that God's revelation of His Creation is not, in fact, unchanging. It too is moving with time.

Why?

Because, God, it seems obviously apparent, had never revealed scientific knowledge to his prophets. Yes, God made Man with the intelligence and ability to, collectively, discover geographic truths, scientific truths, engineering truths, medical truths, etc. and exploit them to advance human civilization, human health, human communication and quality of life. And — this is so important — God has always been determined to present His many revelations to His many prophets in language and concept that fits into each prophet's level of scientific, geographic and biological knowledge during each prophets' lifetime on earth.

What does that mean?

It means that words and concepts given to God's prophets and passed down to us in today's Bible

were chosen to fit within the understood human knowledge of the era when first revealed. And, it is that long-ago, primitive knowledge and terminology that clouds our ability to understand His many revelations. So, our challenge today is to <u>mentally place ourselves in the knowledge basis of thousands of years ago</u> and seek to make sense of the book of Genesis and the other books of the Bible from that perspective.

That is what I have striven to do.

<u>I have placed myself, mentally, into the knowledge basis of thousands of years ago, and then begun to read. In so doing, I have found a pathway that teaches how both God's creation of we humans and subsequent human evolution can be understood with far more agreement than generally thought.</u>

And what about Evolution? How about human evolution following God's creation of Adam and Eve?

I have studied that as well. And I find that human evolution will become far more understandable to us today if we join together our human creation knowledge to our subsequent human evolution knowledge and examine the resulting understanding, which I will call **"unified knowledge."**

My study attempts to do this — to resolve a "unified knowledge" that is derived from an **intelligent and unbiased analysis** of what we humans know about God's creation of Adam and Eve and what we humans today know about our subsequent evolution over 10,000 generations.

One final bit of advice: my study is irrevocably dedicated to seeking the truth, in accordance with the directive by Jesus Christ, who instructed:

In all endeavors seek the truth – *"for the truth shall set you free."*

Best wishes to you, and thanks for reading this study.

Howard Ray White, 86, a devout Christian, long retired professional engineer, author of 21 books in addition to this one, married for 65 years to his beautiful and talented wife.

Chapter 1, God's Creation of the Heavens and Earth

IN THE BEGINNING, GOD CREATED THE UNIVERSE. Astrophysicists tell us that the enormous Universe they observe from earth today is probably the result of a "**Big Bang**" in which mass and energy was hurled from an unbelievably dense mass that had been located at the center of the universe. And, based on the speed at which heavenly bodies appear to be flying apart today, astronomers calculate that the "Big Bang" event had taken place **13,900,000,000 years ago**. God confirms, through his prophet, that He was the Creator of what we call the "Big Bang." The first part of the first sentence in the Torah, as reproduced in the Holy Bible, reports:

In the beginning God created the heavens . . .

As the swirling matter and energy sped outward from the "Big Bang," and cooled, it subdivided into rotating regions that further gathered into rotating galactic discs, which we call galaxies. The swirling matter and energy that was hurled in our direction by the "Big Bang" gathered into the Milky Way Galaxy, and that is the galaxy in which we live. Within the Milky Way Galaxy, matter further cooled and gravitational forces gathered that matter into thousands of rotating stellar discs. In many of those rotating stellar discs, sufficient matter eventually gathered at the center to ignite thermonuclear fusion, and that caused the central mass within that disc to shine as a star. One of these was our Sun and matter was rotating around it.

Perhaps I should tell you how many stars we now believe presently exist in the Universe. Then I will present an estimate of how many grains of sand presently exist in all of the beaches on Earth. Then I will present the United States national debt in pennies. You will find these numbers of interest, for it is the size of God's humongous Universe that is so hard for little human beings like us to comprehend.

- **Total number of stars in the Universe**:

    300,000,000,000,000,000,000,000

- Grains of sand on all of the beaches on Earth:

    4,800,000,000,000,000,000,000

- The U. S. National Debt in pennies (2/12/2023):

    $3,145,836,000,000,000

    and climbing fast!

Let us now consider a long-ago primitive rotating stellar disc such as our then-primitive solar system, which would become the Earth, the Sun and its other planets. It then **looked like a dark region** rotating around our central mass because our central mass was not yet able to shine.   God confirms, through his prophet, how Earth looked at this point, when the earth was primitive and the central mass, our Sun, was not yet shining. The complete first and second sentence in the Bible reports:

16

In the beginning God created the heavens and the earth. Now, the earth was formless and empty, darkness was over the surface of the deep, and the Spirit of God was hovering over the waters.[1]

Since language was limited by primitive scientific understanding at the time God delivered this revelation, "*waters*" was perhaps the word chosen to represent all "fluids," for the heat within primitive Earth's forming mass certainly made that mass a very hot fluid environment. Waters, vapors and atmosphere were all considered fluids. The center of our solar system was to become our "sun," but it had not yet triggered thermonuclear fusion and did not yet shine. Furthermore, clouds of dust and gases on primitive "Earth" also obscured the light from those distant stars that had begun to shine.

So, "*darkness was over the surface of the deep*."

Therefore, we learn that Earth and the other forming primitive planets revolved around our central mass (our future Sun). Also, most planets spun as they revolved around our central mass. Planets had insufficient mass to be stars, but thermonuclear reactions, gravitational forces and meteor and comet impacts caused these forming planets to be very hot and volcanic. It would take a long time for meteor and comet impacts to subside and for

---

[1] All Bible references and quotes are from the Revelations and Matthew books of the Holy Bible, the New International Version.

planets to cool down enough to retain much water or a friendly atmosphere.

Unable to remain at the surface of turbulent planets, incoming water was pushed back out into space, where it spent long periods in the form of ice, and often gathered into comets, or it remained because it became chemically bound within earth's rock.

Now, at some point, our central mass, our Sun, became dense enough to support thermonuclear fusion, and a star was born. **Earth now experienced steady sunshine.** And each rotating planet exposed to that new sunlight experienced sunrises and sunsets – separating the light from the darkness.

Our central mass, the star that gives us life, became what we call the "Sun." Astrophysicists calculate that the Sun began to shine 6,000,000,000 years ago. The planet on which we live, we call "Earth." God confirms through his prophet how Earth looked at this point. The third through the sixth sentences in the Bible report:

> *And God said, "Let there be light," and there was light. God saw that the light was good, and he separated the light from the darkness. God called the light "day," and the darkness he called "night." And there was evening, and there was morning – the first day.*

We now move into "the second day," still mentally limited in our Biblical mind-set to a primitive knowledge because we must read *Genesis* as if we know no more than people knew over 3,000 years ago.

As Earth cooled further, it acquired an atmosphere of nitrogen and carbon dioxide. Initially, there was very little water on Earth, for most existed out in the space occupied by the Sun and her planets, of which Earth was number three. So, there was an expanse of atmosphere, and, beyond that, an expanse of vast space, where ice roamed. Earth was still harsh, and without life.

But the ice attracted to Earth was no longer being pushed back into space, for the Earth had cooled sufficiently for liquid water to accumulate on its surface, and for ice to accumulate at its poles. So, there was water on Earth, and an atmosphere above. But, most of the water we see today on Earth was still out in space, in the form of roaming ice, or to some extent, on Mars. God confirms through his prophet how Earth looked at this point. The seventh through the eleventh sentences in the Bible report:

> *And God said, "Let there be an expanse between the waters to separate water from water." So, God made the expanse and separated the water under the expanse from the water above it. And it was so. God called the expanse "sky." And there was evening, and there was morning – the second day.*

Again, the language available to God's prophet limited how the story of the atmosphere could be revealed. There was no word to distinguish "outer space" from

19

"atmosphere." So, everything above the ground and the seas was "sky."

The presence of water on Earth accelerated the cooling of the surface. As it further cooled, the Earth's crust fractured into tectonic plates, and those plates began to slowly move across the molten core within. New crust steadily emerged through trenches in the young oceans, forming new crust at the edges of the tectonic plates. And, old crust steadily melted away where it dove down at the far edge, where two adjacent plates moved toward each other with terrific force.

So, fresh land was continually being formed beneath the young oceans, and was being conveyed by interior forces toward the beaches, and beyond, **where it became new dry land**. And, the oceans became deeper and more defined, as crust movement became more defined, and as more ice was swept into earth's gravitational field from the space through which it roamed. The action of water and wind erosion and the emergence of land from beneath the oceans produced a primitive soil.

God confirms through his prophet how Earth looked at this point. The twelfth through the fifteenth sentences in the Bible report:

And God said, "Let the water under the sky be gathered to one place, and let dry ground appear." And it was so. God called the dry ground "land," and the gathered waters he called "seas." And God saw that it was good.

Chapter 2, God's Creation of Life

BASED ON TODAY'S ASTRONOMICAL KNOWLEDGE, I must rationalize that, throughout the Universe, there are nurturing planets and moons where life abounds, millions of them. (The Bible does not deny the existence of life elsewhere.) One of these planets where life exists is our Earth.

It was about **4,000,000,000 years ago**, when primitive life began to arrive at Earth and survive, multiplying and replicating itself according to its kind. These primitive life chemicals were arriving in the ice that Earth continually swept from space, especially within an occasional ice-covered meteor, or, much less frequently – within an arriving comet. The first life was much more primitive than today's viruses or bacteria; it was the chemical building blocks of life – what we call **RNA**. RNA survives today as a component within each cell in our body. These first life forms lived under the ice fields of the far north oceans and far south oceans, and drew energy from geothermal flumes rising up from the ocean floor below. The temperature and crystal structure of the impure ice sustained the fragile chemicals of primitive life forms, while, at the same time, the geothermal flumes provided nutrients and energy.

Overhead, the atmosphere was almost totally made up of **carbon dioxide and nitrogen**. There was no significant **oxygen**. And the clouds and atmospheric dust made every day look like a dim cloudy winter day. If we had visited earth at that time, we would not have been able to see anything overhead but dense clouds: no Sun, no Moon, and no stars. As time passed, life within the oceans became more complex and viruses and bacteria appeared. <u>Yet, no life form drew energy from oxygen, for little was present</u>. In fact, life struggled to develop defenses against being destroyed by the little oxygen that did exist, for its presence was increasing.

<u>Photosynthesis</u> had begun. It started with plant life in the oceans. Using the dim sunlight that was penetrating down to the surface of the oceans, some types of single-cell organisms were converting carbon dioxide to oxygen, essential to support animal life.

Yet, animal life had not yet arrived. There was nothing as complex as the smallest minnow, snail or sea-worm. The most successful life forms were the large humps of stromatolite, where colonies of diverse microbes thrived by symbiotic relationships.

But, expanding plant life did not remain confined to the oceans because the floors of the oceans were continually being conveyed, slowly but surely, up and across the beaches by tectonic forces within earth's interior. <u>By riding upon the emerging ocean floors, **plant life came to the dry land**</u>. Exposure to the dryness of land killed almost all of the plant life soon after it emerged from the ocean, but a remnant survived, and strengthened its ability to cope in that harsh environment. In time, these ocean plants developed into primitive land plants.

Now, forces were in place to accelerate changes in the earth's atmosphere. No longer would the atmosphere consist of carbon dioxide and nitrogen, with little oxygen, for much oxygen was being produced by the new land plants and the expanded plant life forms within the ocean waters. The sixteenth through the nineteenth sentences in the Bible report:

> And God said, "Let the land produce vegetation: seed-bearing plants and trees on the land that bear fruit with seed in it, according to their various kinds." And it was so. The land produced vegetation: plants bearing seed according to their kinds, and trees bearing fruit with seed in it according to their kinds. And God saw that it was good. And there was evening, and there was morning – the third day.

By **2,000,000,000 years ago**, there was significant **oxygen** present in the atmosphere. This made possible a new form of life: life that derived its energy by consuming oxygen. Oxygen-consuming life forms would complement the carbon dioxide-consuming life forms that were already abundant, and thereby complete a vital cycle in which these essential life-supporting chemicals would never be depleted. As the atmosphere enriched in oxygen, and the earth matured, the perpetual cloudiness changed to occasional cloudiness. Had man been present on earth at this time, he could have looked up and, for the first time, seen the sun, the moon and the stars.

23

And, God revealed to His prophets the story of this step in His sequence of creation on Earth, but language problems must have confounded the story. (Remember our guiding premise: we must recalibrate our minds back to the primitive knowledge basis that was prevalent thousands of years ago.) <u>Instead of the account being passed down through the generations as "God made the sun, moon and stars visible in the sky," the account was passed down as *"God made the sun, moon and stars and placed them in the sky."*</u>

The twentieth through the twenty-sixth sentences in the Bible report:

> *And God said, "Let there be lights in the expanse of the sky to separate the day from the night, and let them serve as signs to mark seasons and days and years, and let there be lights in the expanse of the sky to give light on the earth." And it was so. God made two great lights – the greater light to govern the day and the lesser light to govern the night. He also made the stars. God set them in the expanse of the sky to give light on earth, to govern the day and the night, and to separate light from darkness. And God saw that it was good. And there was evening, and there was morning – the fourth day.*

At this point Earth had a viable regenerative life cycle, which was based on the vital synergism between plants and animals. **The inexhaustible carbon dioxide-to-oxygen-to-carbon dioxide cycle was now thriving.**

So, new life expanded by leaps and bounds. <u>Occasionally, new ice-bound DNA arrived in meteors and comets, survived the plunge through earth's atmosphere, and further seeded new and unique life forms</u>. Mutations expanded the variations within established life-form families. New life forms proliferated, most noticeably in the oceans, where life had originated. In the oceans, there was a rich concentration of living single-cell life forms on which to base an upward spiraling food chain. So, various fishes and seabirds evolved according to God's plan. Life in the ocean was no longer tiny creatures too small to be seen without a microscope.

By **500,000,000 years ago** the ocean had become home to plants and animals (fishes, etc.) in sizes similar to the more diminutive species we see today. At the height of this era, while nesting on land out of reach of ocean-bound predators, <u>flying reptiles fed off the life forms within the oceans</u>. The twenty-seventh through the thirty-first sentences in the Bible report:

> *And God said, "Let the water teem with living creatures, and let birds fly above the earth across the expanse of the sky." So, God created the great creatures of the sea and every living and moving thing with which the water teems, according to their kinds, and every winged bird according to its kind. And God saw that it was good. God blessed them and said, "Be fruitful and increase in number and fill the water in the seas, and let the birds increase on the earth." And*

there was evening, and there was morning – the fifth day.

So, flying reptiles and primitive birds remained on the land and developed the ability to feed off the growing supply of land plants. And, they went inland to lakes and established themselves there.

Other sea life evolved the ability to crawl, then to walk upon the land, and to migrate far inland. God relied on this evolution to populate the land with many kinds of animals, from small to large.

The dinosaurs arose about **200,000,000 years ago**, but suddenly died off **65,000,000 years ago**, victims of an asteroid or comet collision with Earth.

Yet, that global catastrophe encouraged the evolution of the **mammal species** we see today. Some animals fed on plants. Among those would be the animals that man would eventually domesticate. Others fed on other animals. Some fed on both.

The thirty-eighth through the forty-first sentences in the Bible report:

And God said, "Let the land produce living creatures according to their kinds: livestock, creatures that move along the ground, and wild animals, each according to its kind." And it was so. God made the wild animals according to their kinds, the livestock according to their kinds, and all the creatures that moved along the ground according to their kinds. And God saw that it was good.

Chapter 3, God's Creation of Man

SO, GOD HAD CREATED the heavens and the Earth, and He had created the plants and animals that lived upon the Earth. This He revealed through His prophets and the account has been passed down to us through the first forty-one sentences in the Bible. **God** <u>presented His account in terms of six "phases," which His prophets symbolized as six "days."</u>

The sixth phase yet remained. <u>That last phase would be the creation of man.</u>

Because it is illogical to think otherwise when considering the vastness of the Universe, my understanding is that, throughout the Universe, there are planets and moons where advanced plant and animal ecosystems flourish. I further suspect and submit to you that, when one of these advanced nurturing planets or moons became capable of supporting a being made in the image of God, He quite likely proceeded to create a new community of intelligent beings, each complete with a supernatural soul, and each customized to live in the environment of that site, be it a planet or moon. But that is conjecture. We must confine our search for an understanding closer to home.

It was about 200,000 years ago that God, upon recognizing that Earth was then at an optimum point in evolution, chose to create man.

It is apparent today from fossil records that, for about 2,000,000 years, primate animals and animals that superficially resembled man had been living on earth. Some of the animals that resembled man, which I will call hominid animals, even used crude stone tools. Apparently, the most advanced hominid animals and primate animals lived in east Africa. But these were all animals, I believe. The creation of man would be God's handiwork. Let me postulate below about how it might have been done.

Wisely desiring that man's body share the biology of earthly animals, I suppose that God created man by modifying the DNA structure of a hominid animal or sub-human animal instead of starting anew. As evidence supporting this supposition, I remind you that the nuclear DNA of Neanderthals (probably the most advanced humanoid), based on frozen tissue found in one that died about 40,000 years ago, matches 99.7 percent of the nuclear DNA of modern man, and that today's chimpanzee and today's man share 98.8 percent of the same nuclear DNA structure. I have no insight into how God created the natural side of man, but suggest that He might have inserted man's DNA structure into a barren egg retrieved from the chosen primate or hominid surrogate mother (today's biotechnology science points to that technique). It seems logical for God to use the biochemistry that had evolved on earth, for man was to be compatible with earth's eco-system with regard to diet and resistance to environmental and biological hazards. Furthermore, I suppose God had no reason to want man to be unnecessarily different from the animals on earth with regard to biology. That would have served no useful purpose it seems to me.

So, I suggest that God took an existing hominid or primate animal **DNA** structure and modified it to create an intelligent, athletic being capable of living anywhere on earth, whether hot or cold, dry or wet – a being remarkably advanced in intelligence from any animal that had ever lived on earth – a being capable of elaborate speech and beautiful music – an energetic being with immense capacity for love and hate – but a being whose fragile childhood body was extremely dependent on many years of attentive nurturing.

In addition, I believe God gave man something unique and even more remarkably special beyond the biological gifts. **I believe God gave man a spirit capacity called a soul, for He wanted to be able to later invite the souls of chosen men, women and children into Heaven**.

Again, I remind you that I am presenting my belief to stimulate your thinking on these matters. That God created man and man's soul I am personally convinced, and the Bible says so! Although I have guessed at how He accomplished the natural side of that feat, I have no idea at all how He gave man a supernatural soul.

So, by whatever method God used, in due time, a baby boy was born: the first human. God gave him the name "*Adam*." I would expect that Adam more closely resembled the babies born to African women today than any other modern race. God kept close watch over little Adam. Before many years had passed, God took a few cells from Adam and created the egg for the first female "man," and, if my previous reasoning is applied, He would have planted that egg into a chosen female hominid or primate's womb. That egg grew into the female "man," which God named "*Eve*." As with Adam, God would look over the rearing of Eve. And, with Adam as the father, Eve would later bear children.

The creation of baby Adam and baby Eve, and their rearing and training through both childhood and adulthood, represented God's First Covenant with man, which I will term, God's "*Covenant of Nurture*."

The history of the creation and nurturing of man and woman is presented next.

Chapter 4, God's First Covenant: His Covenant of Nurture — Adam and Eve

GOD WOULD LATER REVEAL TO MAN, through his first prophets, probably in the days of Noah, that He had named the site of man's creation "**Eden**," and that He had named the first male, "**Adam**," and the first female, "Eve." But in Noah's day, the prophets had no knowledge of east Africa south of the Nile - the true first homeland of early man. <u>Therefore, the story of Adam and Eve during its retelling down through subsequent generations became identified as being on the east bank of</u> **Black Lake**. <u>Black Lake would become today's</u> **Black Sea**. That was the home of Noah and his people. Students of geography will recall that the Black Sea is a large body of salt water north of Turkey and south of Ukraine.

Today, we know that the nature of a person is determined by the DNA in each of his or her body cells — a very tiny bit of matter to be sure. <u>Since the prophets had no knowledge of the biology of living cells and their DNA, they would describe that microscopic material as</u> *"**dust of the ground**,"* <u>and they would describe the removed structural piece of Adam's body as a *"rib"*</u>.

<u>What the prophets did not say is important</u>. You see, it is important that we understand that the prophet's presentation of God's creation of man did not make any logical sense to ancient believers. It only makes sense to modern-day scientists! The prophets did not say that God

made a likeness of Adam or Eve out of molded clay or carved stone, and then breathed life into it; did not say that He transformed some animal into Adam and Eve, et cetera. Amazingly, the prophets described DNA as the smallest known particle of matter, a particle so small that it seemed to float in the air – dust. And they **did** choose to tell that Eve was created from a small, dispensable part of Adam's body – a rib. Was this a biological sample of genetic bone or soft tissue? Is that story about surgery? <u>It seems to be a story out of a modern genetics fertility laboratory.</u>

God's prophet reveals the story of God's creation of **Adam and Eve** in the following way:

Then, God said, "Let us make man in our image, in our likeness, and let them rule over the fish of the sea and the birds of the air, over the livestock, over all the earth, and over all the creatures that move along the ground." So God created man in His own image, in the image of God He created him; male and female He created them.

So, the Lord God caused the man to fall into a deep sleep; and while he was sleeping, He took one of the man's ribs and closed up the place with flesh. Then the Lord God made a woman from the rib He had taken out of the man, and He brought her to the man.

Adam named his wife Eve, because she would become the mother of all the living.

The man said, "This is now bone of my bones and flesh of my flesh; she shall be called 'woman,' for she was taken out of man."

God blessed them and said to them, "Be fruitful and increase in number; fill the earth and subdue it. Rule over the fish of the sea and the birds of the air and over every living creature that moves on the ground."

Then, God said, "I give you every seed-bearing plant on the face of the whole earth and every tree that has fruit with seed in it. They will be yours for food. And to all the beasts of the earth and all the birds of the air and all the creatures that move on the ground – everything that has the breath of life in it – I give every green plant for food." And it was so.

God saw all that He had made, and it was very good. And there was evening, and there was morning – the sixth day.

Having discussed God's creation of Adam and Eve, we move on. At this point going forward, evolutionary forces influence outcomes.

During God's *Covenant of Nurture*, Adam and Eve's clan grew to several generations. Yet, it seems obvious to me, they continued to be totally dependent on God and his angels for their survival, because they had no one else to teach them coping skills and parents had to raise children. One can imagine that members of the clan were bonded to God and his angels in a manner resembling the way a

35

servant might have been bonded to his master a few hundred years ago. The servant had limited freedom and, in exchange, the master was totally responsible for the welfare of the servant and his family. During this formative period, men and women were obligated to honor God, to be subservient to God, and follow the rules of conduct God had taught them. They were expected to suppress creative thinking about what ought to be considered "good," and what ought to be considered "evil."

God taught Adam's clan the beginnings of language. Perhaps, God began that process by first encouraging man to give names to the plants and animals he encountered, and to remember those names. Perhaps God taught man to make fire and cook meat. He probably taught man how to build crude huts, and how to make clothing from animal skins and from woven grasses, tied with vines or strips of bark. Surely, God taught man how to make spears and club weapons to enable males to defend the clan from wild animals and hominid animals (animals that resembled man).

Yes, it seems apparent that God had a lot invested in Adam and Eve and their clan of children, grandchildren, great grandchildren, etc. He realized that, at man's creation, mankind was perhaps the most fragile being on earth. Consider how babies today are dependent on parents for at least five years, not capable of being independent until after, say, 13 or more. If Adam's clan was killed off, God knew that He would have to start over by creating another baby Adam.

God's prophet reveals to us the story of how God used the creation site in east Africa, Eden, to nurture Adam, Eve, and their immediate descendants. (Modern scientific exploration makes us comfortable in placing Eden in East Africa.) But, where did His prophet place "in the east of Eden" on the map of the then-known world, as reported in the Bible? The site was not placed in Africa, because that region was not known to the people to whom the prophet was speaking. No, **Eden** was confused with geography closer to each prophet's home.

A few pages further into this study you will arrive at the story of **Noah and the Great Flood**. We have a preview of that story just below, where you read about four noteworthy rivers that are associated with Eden. After reading the account of Noah a few pages later in this study, you might want to return here to the story of Eden for a second interpretation.

If so, then consider the possibility that God's prophet and later generations confused the actual site of Adam and Eve's homeland with Noah's original homeland on the shores of Black Lake, now the Black Sea, and with Abraham's homeland in the Tigris and Euphrates Valley.

Perhaps, the **Gihon**, a word meaning "spurter," was a river feeding Black Lake, such as the Danube, and perhaps the **Pishon**, a word meaning "gusher," was the Bosporus floodwater pouring into Black Lake. Perhaps, the **Tigris** and **Euphrates** rivers were added to the story after the catastrophic flooding had driven many Black Lake people, such as Noah's family, to Mesopotamia. Perhaps, the four rivers symbolize a family tree, a history of a people, whereby the ancestral rivers, Gihon and Pishon, flow forward in time, to create the descendant rivers, Tigris and Euphrates. I am sorry if this is confusing. It will make more sense later.

The prophets' account of Eden begins as follows:

Now the Lord God had planted a <u>garden in the east of Eden</u>; and there He put the man He had formed. And the Lord God made all kinds of trees grow out of the ground – trees that were pleasing to the eye and good for food. In the middle of the garden were the tree of life and the tree of the knowledge of good and evil.

A river watering the garden flowed from Eden; from there it was separated into four headwaters. The name of the first is the Pishon; it winds through the entire land of Havilah, where there is gold. (The gold of that land is good; aromatic resin and onyx are also there.) The name of the second river is the Gihon; it winds through the entire land of Cush. The name of the third river is the Tigris; it runs along the east side of Asshur. And the fourth river is the Euphrates.

The Lord God took the man and put him in the Garden of Eden to work it and take care of it. And, the Lord God commanded the man, "You are free to eat from any tree in the garden; but you must not eat from the tree of the knowledge of good and evil, for when you eat of it you will surely die."

After a few generations were born, and Adam's clan had attained a size and a level of skill that God believed would be sufficient for man-kind's survival, He prepared to set man free from His close oversight. Now, being free meant that God and His angels would not be hovering nearby ready to rush in to deflect danger from outside the clan, to settle an internal squabble within the clan, to circumvent a food shortage, to deal with a severe cold spell, or to help rebuild a hut. Man would have to grapple with good and evil by coping with issues himself. Supernatural help from God and His angels would be much more remote.

It seems to me that God wanted to stress this change in the relationship between Himself and man in a symbolic way. The story of that symbolism is handed down, by God's revelation through his prophets, as the story of the tree of good and evil that grew in the center of a garden that God had prepared in the eastern part of a region named "Eden."

A quick read of that story implies that the first man, Adam, and the first woman, Eve, were the two people who acquired knowledge of good and evil, and that event preceded the birth of any children to the couple. However, I am persuaded that the revelation of this event to one of God's Prophets, because it preceded the invention of written language, became garbled in its retelling down through the generations. Since the name **Adam also means "man,"** and the name **Eve also means "woman,"** the story of how men and women were made independent of God's immediate oversight and nurturing became confused with the names of the first couple, Adam and Eve.

<u>So, it was at the garden in the east of Eden that God revealed to mankind that he was making the descendants of Adam and Eve independent.</u>

From that point on, men and women would have to cope without benefit of God's immediate and personal help. With few exceptions, **God was retreating to a spiritual background from which He would only be accessible through prayer**.

In the following way, God's prophet revealed the story of how our Lord God made Adam and Eve's clan independent:

> *Now, the serpent was more crafty than any of the wild animals the Lord God had made. He said to the woman, "Did God really say, 'You must not eat from any tree in the garden'?"*
>
> *The woman said to the serpent, "We may eat fruit from the trees in the garden, but God did say, 'You must not eat fruit from the tree that is in the middle of the garden, and you must not touch it, or you will die'."*
>
> *"You will not surely die," the serpent said to the woman. "For God knows that when you eat of it your*

eyes will be opened, and you will be like God, knowing good and evil."

When the woman saw that the fruit of the tree was good for food and pleasing to the eye, and also desirable for gaining wisdom, she took some and ate it. She also gave some to her husband, who was with her, and he ate it. Then the eyes of both of them were opened, and they realized they were naked; so they sewed fig leaves together and made coverings for themselves.

Then the man and his wife heard the sound of the Lord God as he was walking in the garden in the cool of the day, and they hid from the Lord God among the trees of the garden. But the Lord God called to the man, "Where are you?"

He answered, "I heard you in the garden, and I was afraid because I was naked; so I hid."

And he said, "Who told you that you were naked? Have you eaten from the tree that I commanded you not to eat from?"

The man said, "The woman you put here with me – she gave me some fruit from the tree, and I ate it."

Then the Lord God said to the woman, "What is this you have done?"

The woman said, "The serpent deceived me, and I ate."

So, the Lord God said to the serpent, "Because you have done this, cursed are you above all the livestock and all the wild animals! You will crawl on your belly and you will eat dust all the days of your life. And I will put enmity between you and the woman, and between your offspring and hers; he will crush your head, and you will strike his heel."

To the woman he said, "I will greatly increase your pains in childbearing; with pain you will give birth to children. Your desire will be for your husband, and he will rule over you."

To Adam he said, "Because you listened to your wife and ate from the tree about which I commanded you, 'You must not eat it,' cursed is the ground because of you; through painful toil you will eat of it all the days of your life. It will produce thorns and thistles for you, and you will eat the plants of the field. By the sweat of your brow you will eat your food until you return to the ground, since from dust you are and to dust you will return."

The Lord God made garments of skin for Adam and his wife and clothed them. And the Lord God said, "The man has now become like one of us, knowing good and evil. He must not be allowed to reach out his hand and take also from the tree of life and eat, and live forever." So, the Lord God banished him from the Garden of Eden to work the ground from which he had been taken. After He drove the man out, He placed on *the east side of the Garden of Eden cherubim and a flaming sword flashing back and forth to guard the way to the tree of life.*

We have now arrived at a major transition.

In reading the story of this transition, it is helpful to realize that the prophet's story of God's day-to-day guidance and oversight over Adam and Eve and the first few subsequent generations of mankind had been shortened to just a few years. <u>Our logical mind realizes that close supernatural guidance over the first few generations of mankind would have been necessary for that first clan to become capable of successful living.</u>

At this point, God Almighty discarded His *Covenant of Nurture.*

In its place, He established a new covenant.

I will call this period, *God's "Covenant of Tough Love."*

Why Tough Love? Because God knew he was intentionally forcing Adam and Eve's descendants to cope, on their own, with a multitude of unpredictable hardships over a span of 200,000 years from that time to present times.

Chapter 5, God's Second Covenant: His Covenant of Tough Love — Eden

THERE IS COMPELLING SCIENTIFIC EVIDENCE supporting the dating of man's creation, and locating that event in east Africa.

Fairly recently, geneticists have been able to calculate that God's creation of Adam and Eve occurred about **200,000 years ago**. That calculation is based on the pattern of variations presently occurring around the world in the structure of human **mitochondrial DNA**.

Mitochondrial DNA exists outside of the cell's nucleus in organelles, from where it directs the energy functions within the cell. Mitochondrial DNA is not part of the 47-gene DNA that exists in the nucleus of every human cell — what we call "nuclear DNA."

Let us digress and explain. **Nuclear DNA** is the molecular structure that contains the complete genetic code that makes every human a unique, one-of-a-kind individual (except for identical twins). Nuclear DNA is the result of the combination at conception of the DNA structure in the awaiting female egg, and the DNA structure of the successful male sperm.

In contrast, **mitochondrial DNA** is already present in the awaiting female egg, and is unaltered by the male sperm. Therefore, the structure of mitochondrial DNA is passed to offspring only by the mother. Like nuclear DNA, mitochondrial DNA occasionally undergoes mutations, and these mutations are passed onto offspring.

This means that mitochondrial DNA's "from-mother-only" feature greatly facilitates a study of patterns in human origin and migration.

These mitochondrial studies show that there are relatively few mutational differences among people today, whether they are Africans, Asians, Europeans, Native Americans, or even Pygmies or Australian Aborigines – all of we humans belong to the same close genetic family. Let me repeat: all of we humans belong to the same close genetic family

There are two main branches to that family – the **Africa branch** and the **Out-of-Africa branch** (which actually includes some people living in Africa).

The oldest branch is the Africa branch, for it contains many more mutations than the Out-of-Africa branch. These observations and other studies indicate that God created man at some spot in Africa. And man seems to be a newcomer on earth, showing only one-tenth the mitochondrial variation that is present in our closest living genetic relative, the chimpanzee.

This small human mitochondrial DNA variation indicates that man's creation occurred about 200,000 years ago.

Perhaps a footnote is appropriate regarding today's intellectual controversy between scientists who draw conclusions from the fossil record, and scientists who draw conclusions from the genetic variation among present-day people.   Defending their advocacy of reliance on genetic patterns among the living, geneticists Allan Wilson and Rebecca Cann wrote in *Scientific American*: "Living genes must have ancestors, whereas dead fossils may not have descendants. Molecular biologists therefore know the genes they are examining must have been passed through lineages that survived to the present; paleontologists cannot be sure that the fossils they examine do not lead down an evolutionary blind alley."

It seems that man spent the first **90,000 years** of his 200,000-year existence-to-date living in Africa. There he procreated, experienced expanding diversity through evolution, and learned to defend against wild animals, to gather nuts, fruits and grains, to hunt animals for meat, to maintain interpersonal relations, and, most importantly, to exterminate the animals that most closely resembled him – the hominids.

Apes, chimpanzees and monkeys did not compete very much with man, so they consequently escaped his war-like nature. Not so homo erectus and other creatures we call hominids – creatures like the Neanderthal and those in Olduvai Gorge, whose fossil records have been so well publicized by the Leakeys and *National Geographic* magazine. Man was killing them off to the last creature.

Only the **Neanderthals**, the last of the hominids, located much further away to the north would remain for many more years until their final extinction.

By the end of that first 90,000-year period, man had congregated into villages, and had built temples to God.

Instead of ranging far and wide, man was settling down amid the comforts of east Africa. Although God had commanded Adam and Eve's descendants to procreate and populate the whole earth, they were still clinging to their original home in Africa. There was still plenty of room in Africa, and it seems man had not yet acquired the explorer's drive. Furthermore, the earth's climate had been rather cold over the first **90,000 years** of man's existence and migrating northward would have made survival far more difficult.

Then, a brief warm period emerged that lasted a few thousand years. One would think that this warm weather alone would have encouraged man to venture out of Africa. But, even then, man did not want to leave Africa. So, at this point, God applied pressure to push man out of Africa. Later, He would reveal that event to His prophets, and they have passed the story down to us.

The most dramatic event – the story passed down to us – took place at a town where Adam and Eve's descendants were building an unusually tall mud-brick tower in praise of God, and to bring glory to their village, one would suppose. **It was called the tower of Babel**.

48

They obviously wanted to build a grand city and settle down there, **but God wanted them to disperse across the Earth**. <u>So, God dispersed them by confusing their language and setting them against each other</u>.

The Biblical account says this:

> *"Now the whole world had one language and a common speech. As people moved eastward, they found a plain in Sinar and settled there.*

> *"They said to each other, 'Come, let's make bricks and bake them thoroughly.' They used brick instead of stone, and tar for mortar. Then they said, 'Come, let us build ourselves a city, with a tower that reaches to the heavens, so then we may make a name for ourselves; otherwise, we will be scattered over the face of the whole earth.'*

> *"But the Lord came down to see the city and the tower the people were building. The Lord said, 'If as one people speaking the same language, they have begun to do this, then nothing they plan to do will be impossible for them. Come, let us go down and confuse their language so they will not understand each other.'*

> *"So, the Lord scattered them from there over the earth, and they stopped building the city. That is why it was called Babel – because there the Lord confused the language of the whole world. From*

there the Lord scattered them over the face of the whole earth."

The above Bible story symbolizes God's desire to push some of mankind out of Africa, even though most would still be allowed to stay behind in their ancestral homeland. Man's reluctance to venture into the unknown is understandable. After all, burly and strong hominids lived outside of Africa – the **Neanderthals**.

Neanderthals lived along the essential out-of-Africa pathway: from the eastern boundary of present-day Egypt, across today's Middle East, northward through today's Turkey and into Europe, and eastward through today's Iran and into Asia. **To migrate out of Africa, man had to move into the land of the Neanderthal**.

But, about **110,000 years ago** some did just that. Enough of mankind went out of Africa to satisfy God's plan to implement important diversification through subsequent evolution.

Now, let's discuss the dispersal of man and the evolution of the races of man.

Again, I am presenting my view of this history, but from this point forward, I can advise that it is supported by substantial scientific evidence.

Leaving Africa about 110,000 years ago, man first settled in the region we now call the **Middle East**. Although the migration out of Africa was a small percentage of the population, man left in sufficient numbers to eventually, over may thousands of years, populate all of the other continents.

Leaving the Middle East, man continued on to the east and even to the north. By 60,000 years ago, man was in India and Asia. By 40,000 years ago man was in Indonesia and Australia. By 35,000 years ago, man had populated Europe, even into the northern reaches of Scotland and Norway. By 30,000 years ago, man had crossed over the Bearing land bridge, and begun the first wave into North and South America.

But this migration was not a continuous and pleasant event, because during 80,000 years of this out of Africa 110,000-year period, (between 100,000 and 20,000 years ago), the most-northern faction of mankind had become entrapped in a progressively worsening Ice Age. People who had ventured north of the Alps, the Himalayas, and the intervening mountain chains in Europe and Asia, had become trapped between the expanding northern ice cap and the glacier-covered mountains to the south, which their ancestors had crossed when heading north during warmer times.

Most of them died from exposure, but a remnant won pitched battles for possession of caves, and, in the caves, survivors stubbornly endured for generation after generation. <u>The most dramatic cave-entrance battles occurred between man and the Neanderthal hominids.</u>

Humans and Neanderthal were very similar genetically: 99.7 percent of their nuclear DNA

structure matched. So, man and Neanderthal must have shared some of the same diseases and tendencies toward certain genetic mutations. In fact, recent genetic testing of Neanderthal bones, reported in scientific journals in 2010, suggests that a few Neanderthal-matching genes have been found to have been added to Out-of-Africa-Man's nuclear DNA structure after contact with Neanderthal in the Middle East and northward. These few matches might be the result of limited gene transfer from Neanderthal to humans through sexual union, or be the result of exposure to the same caves and the same environment, which had encouraged independent mutations of the observed matching genes, those mutations proving good for Neanderthal and also good for man.

On the other hand, the same genetic testing indicates that Neanderthal did not acquire genetic mutations that matched to man. So. the matches, few in number, were man matching Neanderthal, not Neanderthal matching man. Approximately one in every fifty genetic variations among Europeans and Asians had a match in Neanderthal. So, the genetic influence was small.

However, those Neanderthal matches are uniformly present in Europeans and Asians. <u>Yet Africans almost never show evidence of those Neanderthal matches. This is an example of a few of the genetic differences that distinguish Africans from Out-of-Africans (Europeans and Asians).</u>

No matches were found between Neanderthal mitochondrial DNA and Out-of-Africa human mitochondrial DNA. Since mitochondrial DNA passes, from mother to child, this lack of any matches suggests that the rape of women by Neanderthal males, if it did produce a viable female baby, resulted in a female baby that was rejected by the mother's clan, or that female baby, if accepted as a girl, was later infertile or was later rejected by human males and did not procreate in significant numbers.

Why did the people who remained in Africa not acquire these few genes mentioned above, which were common to Neanderthals? It was either because there was no sexual union; because they were not exposed to Neanderthal caves or its environment, or because those particular mutations were not good for Africans. So, from the outset of man's migration out of Africa, there were a few genetic changes that matched Neanderthal, and those changes persist in today's European and today's Asian races. But again, those matching gene variations were very few.

The Neanderthal was naturally better adapted to the cold than was man. It was muscular and heavy-set. It had more hair, though it still needed the warmth of the caves it had possessed for many generations. **Neanderthal had their caves; man needed them.** But man could wrestle a Neanderthal about as well as he could wrestle a bear, so one-on-one was not the chosen battle tactic. Although not as strong, man could run faster, a great help when escaping from a bad battle match-up. So, a group of cunning men could entrap one to three Neanderthal males out on the hunt, and eventually severely deplete the number of males living in a cave. Then, they could launch a successful direct attack on the cave and slaughter the females and their young.

So, by group effort, cunning tactics and persistence, man gained possession of essential Neanderthal caves. Over thousands of years, the Neanderthal population, the last of the hominids, diminished under intense pressure from man. Man was exterminating the remnant of remaining Neanderthals. The winners in the struggle for the best home sites were the survivors who had won possession of Ice Age cave habitats. Although perhaps inferior in strength compared to Neanderthals, these survivors were more determined; more cunning; more persistent, and more likely to raise children with those characteristics.

By 30,000 years ago Neanderthal was extinct or very nearly extinct, a victim of man's war-like nature and his cunning, group-effort battle tactics.

But, man's population in the cold northern climes was also reduced, particularly among the less determined, less cunning, less persistent individuals. Consistently then, over thousands of years, a remnant of man survived in the caves of the northern climes. The survivors were the ones who were most determined, most cunning, most persistent, and most adept at coping with the harsh environment. Those traits helped them survive to raise successful families. Athletic skills were less important to survival in the cold northern environment than they were in Africa, so athletic skills became somewhat secondary.

Now, dark-skinned beings living in caves lose the pigmentation in their skin.

That is true of fish, crawfish, crickets, beetles, and salamanders. It is also true of man. I know, because I was an avid cave explorer in my youth. Although the men donned furs and ventured out on hunts, the women largely remained behind in the cave. And the children spent many years almost entirely inside the cave. What little sunlight children received produced more vitamin D within the bodies of the lighter-skinned children, and this contributed to succeeding generations losing their skin pigmentation.

In fact, by 32,000 years ago, long before the last Ice Age cycle abated, descendants of light-skinned, cave-dwelling survivors in the upper Danube Valley in Europe had developed the essential textile skills that were so vital to catching fish and small game, and keeping warm. Some were making needles and fish hooks; rope, nets and fishing cord; blankets, cloth, bags, mats and wall coverings.

So, when earth's weather began to gradually return to the weather we normally experience today – a process that began 20,000 years ago – white-skinned man emerged from the caves of central Europe and light-yellow-skinned man emerged from the caves of northwest China. These two races of men, although at that time extremely small in population, would procreate with outstanding success and dominate the world.

Back in Africa, man had remained mostly isolated from the people who had left that continent 110,000 years ago. African man had expanded to south Africa and to west Africa, but had still made little effort to move north into Europe or northeast into Asia.

On the other hand, as warmer times arrived and the light-skinned cave-dwelling survivors moved southward and crossed over the Southern European mountains and expanded their territory southward, they forced from the best land those dark-skinned people who, during the Ice Age, had enjoyed the luxury of living in the milder southern climates.

Around **14,000 years ago**, warm weather returned in northeast Asia and northwest North America, that being at the end of the last Ice Age. Fortunately, the oceans were still rather low. Those low ocean levels allowed man to migrate eastward and walk over the land bridge that connected northeast Asia to northwest North America, which then existed between those two continents. **This migration of Northeastern Asian man into North America from northeast Asia occurred about 14,000 years ago.** Well, the land bridge soon flooded and prevented further migration eastward to North America. This is the good news: Native American man thrived in his new homeland, from far north to far south, with greater ease than perhaps anywhere else on Earth.

In the Americas, there were no hominid animals like Neanderthal to be killed, and no close relatives like the chimpanzee in whose bodies dangerous viruses and bacteria could adapt for new attacks upon the health of man. In fact, because of man's previous journey through northeast Asia and through northwest North America had taken many years, and had involved passage through very cold climate, their prolonged trek had "acted as a disease filter," so that "most of the illnesses which afflicted men in the Old World were left behind."

Game was plentiful, and animals were not accustomed to defending themselves against man. So, man experienced a huge population explosion as he advanced southward along the Pacific coast, through Central America, and on into South America. And, he moved eastward across mountains and deserts to arrive in eastern North America, where he likewise thrived. Furthermore, he crossed the jungles to reach southeastern South America, and there, too, he found a healthy climate.

And, large game animals fell before man's advance, notable species being killed to extinction. Victims included the mammoth, the horse, the camel, the ground sloth, and a relative of the American bison. By 9,000 years ago, these were all extinct. Yet, the American bison, elk, moose and deer remained, deer being the most useful game animal in southeastern North America.

Once man's expansion from northeast Asia to northwest America began in earnest, he perhaps completed his occupation of **North and South America** within one thousand years, for he found little to impede his advance. Man seemed to be present throughout the Americas by 9,000 years ago.

But, as each generation was born, less and less resistance to Old World diseases remained. However, about 8,500 years later, Columbus discovered the Americas.

Sadly, for all Native American people, they suddenly and desperately needed for their bodies to fight those Old World diseases. But their biological defenses remembered not how.

So, beginning in 1500 A. D., Native American people would die by the millions as Spanish invaders, based in the Caribbean and the Gulf of Mexico, unknowingly dispensed upon a helpless people wave after wave of small pox, measles, typhus, tuberculosis, chicken pox, and influenza.

The above event represents a very sad example of how great suffering can occur because of expanding diversity through evolution.

This now concludes the history of how man spread across the Earth and, in the process, diversified into races. We understand that this human expansion that followed

God's creation of Adam and Eve was an evolutionary process.

Now, let's return to my thoughts on the role that God must have played in this great expansion, this great migration. <u>Since, at about 10,000 years ago, man had spread throughout the earth and eliminated all hominid animals, this was most probably the time that God decided to make a new covenant with man.</u>

Perhaps, I should recap *"The Christian History of God's Humans, from Adam to Today"* up to this point:

About 200,000 years ago, God created man and nurtured the immediate descendants of Adam and Eve, protected them, and taught them survival skills.

Then, perhaps 1,000 years later, God backed off and let man fend for himself, develop advanced food gathering skills and social group-effort skills and wrestling with good and evil as best he could.

Then, at about 110,000 years ago, God felt the need to push man out of Africa, for, in spite of the fact that the weather to the north had become warm, man, for the most part, seemed far too content to stay put in environmentally friendly eastern Africa.

However, during this protracted warm weather cycle, a significant number of mankind did move out of Africa, and populated much of India, Asia and Europe over many decades. But later, a progressively worsening ice age trapped the people that had been lured into the unusually warm northern climes.

Those trapped in the cold north, who were lucky enough to conquer cave sites, took refuge within, and that remnant <u>survived to multiply and become the two most successful races among the races of man, the result of natural human evolution</u>.

We are ready to now advance to the age of Noah. Our next chapter will be called God's "Covenant of Adoption – Noah."

Chapter 6, God's Third Covenant: His Covenant of Adoption — Noah

THE TIME WAS APPROACHING when God would advance to a new covenant, which I will call, His *Covenant of Adoption*. To understand this event, you need to know some meaningful background information. **So, I began this segment with the story of Black Lake.**

During the latter ice age times, **white-skinned man was attracted southward to the edge of Black Lake**, a somewhat salty, land-bound lake centered on today's Black Sea. Back then, Black Lake lay within a huge basin that sloped down to the water, whose surface was then about 500 feet below sea level. Being at such a low altitude, the land around Black Lake was relatively warm, considering its latitude.

But man had to continually retreat, because Black Lake was rapidly filling with glacier salt-free melt. It eventually rose several hundred feet above sea level before it breached the headwaters of the Sakarya River and began overflowing into the Mediterranean Sea. This flushed out all of the salty water.

By 15,000 years ago, the great northern ice cap had retreated so far north that alternate pathways developed which sent the melt water to the North Sea. Furthermore, about 12,500 years ago, the weather became colder and much dryer. As a result of these two changes, the water flowing into Black Lake fell below the rate at which water was evaporating from the surface – the overflow into the

Mediterranean Sea at Sakarya River stopped, and the lake surface began to fall. But the lake water had been so thoroughly flushed free of salt that the concentrating effect of that evaporation did not even make the lake water brackish.

There was another cold, dry spell 8,200 years ago, but it moderated after 400 years.

Finally, two hundred years further brings us to the days of Noah, a man in whom God was especially pleased. Noah lived at the edge of Black Lake 7,600 years ago. This was long before any written language existed on Earth or the start of the rise of Egypt.

The people around Black Lake in the days of Noah were accomplished farmers and fishermen. They cultivated wheat and barley and herded domesticated goats. They built boats and fished the lake. They built houses of differing designs. They traded between villages. They may have even smelted copper, because 6,500-year-old evidence of that technology can be found today from the nearby Balkans southward to Israel.

In fact, the Black Lake people undoubtedly represented the most advanced civilization on earth at that time.

And it appears that, in the days of Noah, 7,600 years ago, **God was ready to reveal Himself more directly to man. The time for harvesting souls was arriving.**

God wanted to make a covenant with a family, so that, through them and their descendants, His presence would be revealed to others. He wanted to make a new and special covenant. For this purpose, **He chose Noah**! Why? Because, among all of the families on Earth, Noah's family stood out as the most righteous and the most capable of becoming God's prophet to future generations.

And, Noah lived in the most advanced civilization on Earth – the shore of Black Lake, where a dramatic event was about to occur.

In the days of Noah, the Sea of Marmara, which was connected to the Mediterranean Sea by the Dardanelle Straight, had, for about 12,500 years, been rising along with all of Earth's oceans in tandem with the melting ice and receding glaciers.

And, the salt water within the Sea of Marmara was only prevented from plunging down into Black Lake by the earthen hills through which the narrow Bosporus Straight now cuts. Those low hills, which had no underpinning of bedrock, lay atop the eastward-creeping Eurasian Plate, near its fault-line junction with the westward-creeping Anatolian Plate.

God knew that, one day, an earthquake would rip those low hills apart, creating a channel through which ocean water in the Mediterranean Sea could rapidly flood Black Lake.

Once the route would become established, erosion would expand the flow hourly. Within days, the flow would be gushing violently. The flow would soon equal that of 200 Niagara Falls. Black Lake would rise six inches every day. Some people living along the shore would see the danger and steadily move back. But many would figure the rising would stop, and would cling to shrinking high ground (islands within Black Lake) too long, only to find their escape route cut off.

Black Lake valley would be flooded within a very few months.

God planned to use this event, which he knew was about to occur, to destroy the most advanced civilization of the day; destroy their homes, farms and way of life; turn their beautiful fresh-water lake into a salt-water sea of death and destruction; force them onto the barren hills beyond; scatter survivors far and wide. God planned to use that event to separate Noah and his family from all of their neighbors, and from the other clans in the valley.

This event would be the Great Flood, which is recorded in several ancient oral histories and in *The Bible*.

So, God came to Noah and told him to prepare for a great flood by building a huge boat according to the set of construction plans that He laid out before the surely dumbfounded man. How could there be such an enormous flood, Noah must have asked? But God assured him that it would take place, and the huge boat was essential to his survival and his immediate family's survival. Asking for Noah's obedience, without benefit of physical evidence of compelling danger, was God's way of testing Noah's faith.

While neighbors laughed at the hard-working Noah, he and his sons struggled to gather the building materials and construct the huge craft. God could have saved Noah and his family with a much smaller craft, but He wanted Noah and his sons to work especially hard at building a really huge craft. It also seems that God wanted to impress man with his upcoming responsibility, as caretaker of life on earth, for the boat was to hold many animals, some of them quite large.

God knew that man's upcoming population explosion would threaten the viability of plants and animals all over the world. Noah's experience was to be a lesson to man: Noah would be the example of a loving caretaker of earth's plants and animals, just as God had always been the loving caretaker of man.

From the Bible we read:

Noah did everything, just as God commanded him.

The Lord then said to Noah, "Go into the ark, you and your whole family, because I have found you righteous in this generation. Take with you seven of every kind of clean animal, a male and its mate, and two of every kind of unclean animal, a male and its mate, and also seven of every kind of bird, male and female, to keep their various kinds alive throughout the earth. Seven days from now, I will send rain on the earth for forty days and forty nights, and I will wipe from the face of the earth every living creature I have made."

After the earthquake produced the fracture, through which seawater broke through the Bosporus hills, Black Lake Valley began to rapidly flood. Although Noah experienced considerable rain, the lake was rising so fast that Noah figured most of the water had to be coming up from springs beneath the ground.

The Bible account says:

"On that day all the springs of the great deep burst forth, and the floodgates of the heavens were opened."

But Noah was prepared for the great flood. His boat was complete, and God had helped with gathering up animals. Noah, his immediate family, the animals, and food for all, were safely aboard Noah's huge boat by the time the water rose up around it. All passengers would stay aboard throughout the remaining filling of the Black Sea.

Eventually, the flooding stopped. *The Bible* says:

"Now the springs of the deep and the floodgates of the heavens had been closed, and the rain had stopped falling from the sky."

Finally, the huge boat drifted to dry ground in the vicinity of Mount Ararat. There, Noah, his family and the animals disembarked.

Before long, Noah must have encountered people and animals that he surely realized had not been aboard the huge boat, but that realization was lost in the retelling of Noah's story down through the generations.

Yes, as the story of the Great Flood was verbally passed down for many generations, for about two to three thousand years, the surviving version of the story of that Great Flood was finally written down to eventually be printed in today's Bible.

The recorded version of the Great Flood was said to have killed all land animals and all people throughout earth, save those in Noah's huge boat.

Many were surely killed by the flood, including thousands of people, and the environmental destruction rent upon the land around Black Lake was obviously complete and total. But, by the time of the Great Flood, man had migrated around the globe, even to North and South America.

The story of the death by drowning of all the people, animals and birds trapped around Black Lake became the story of the alleged death by drowning of all the people and animals living all over the earth. That expansion of scope is easy to understand given that, in those days, a person's knowledge of geography was limited to his immediate region.

Because of Noah's faithfulness prior to the Great Flood, God made a covenant with him. Through Noah and his descendants, God pledged to shepherd a great people, and those people would be the conduits through which God would reveal Himself to man throughout the world. Noah's descendants would become the Jewish people, and Israel would eventually become their homeland.

God's prophet reveals to us the story of how God made his covenant with Noah and his family:

Then, Noah built an altar to the Lord and, taking some of all the clean animals and clean birds, he sacrificed burnt offerings on it. The Lord smelled the pleasing aroma and said in His heart: "Never again will I curse the ground because of man, even though every inclination of his heart is evil from childhood. And never again will I destroy all living creatures, as I have done." . . .

"Whoever sheds the blood of man, by man shall his blood be shed; for in the image of God has God made man."

"As for you, be fruitful and increase in number; multiply on the earth and increase upon it."

Then, God said to Noah and to his sons with him: "I now establish my covenant with you and with your descendants after you and with every living creature that was with you – the birds, the livestock and all the wild animals, all those that came out of the ark with you – every living creature on earth. I establish my covenant with you: Never again will all life be cut off by the waters of a flood; never again will there be a flood to destroy the earth."

Survivors of the destruction of the Black Lake region would migrate to other regions, taking with them the skills they had developed in what had been man's most advanced civilization:

Farmers, called Vinca, would move into the plains of present-day Bulgaria. Others would migrate into present-day Greece. People called Linearbandkeramik would flee up the Dniester River, and on across Europe as far as present-day Paris. Others would move up the Dnieper, the Don and the Volga rivers into Russia. Others would flee east to the Caspian Sea and domesticate the horse, with which they would master the huge expanse of Asian land to the east.

A group, perhaps looking for a place to apply their irrigation farming skills, would migrate south past the Mediterranean and into the Nile Valley, where they would lead in the expansion of Egyptian civilization.

But many, including **Noah's family**, would travel south-southeast across the mountains into the Tigris and Euphrates Valley, where they would establish irrigation-based farming where practical.

Eventually, Noah's descendants would move further downstream to the delta region and contribute to the great Sumerian Civilization.

That is the story of Noah, which most of you have heard before, but probably not in the manner that I have just presented it. By the way, there is a growing body of new and exciting scientific evidence to support my assertion that Noah's flood occurred at Black Lake 7,600 years ago.

God's covenant with Noah was His third Covenant, which I had named, God's *"Covenant of Adoption – Noah."*

Why? Because, with this covenant God signaled that He was adopting the Jewish people, so that He would be revealed to mankind through them.

This was the first of three covenants that God would make with His Adopted People, the Jews. As mentioned earlier, Noah's people would cross the mountains of present-day Turkey, and make their way to the Euphrates delta.

In that land, 3,500 years later, God would speak to Abram.

Yes, about 4,100 years ago, God made another covenant with man. He made a covenant with Abram, who he renamed **Abraham**. Abram was a descendant of Noah.

70

This was God's fourth covenant, which I shall call, God's *"Covenant of Expanding Presence – Abraham to Moses."*

AT THE TIME GOD INITIATED HIS COVENANT OF EXPANDING PRESENCE, Abram lived in the city of Ur, in the land of the Chaldeans (in present-day southern Iraq). <u>God told Abram to leave the land of his people and migrate to Canaan</u> (in present-day Israel) – a new land that was destined to become the land of God's Jewish Nation, His first people.

Abram obeyed God and moved to the land of Canaan. There, God gave Abram land. By the way, shortly thereafter, God revealed His wrath toward sinful people, for, before Abram's eyes, the people of **Sodom and Gomorrah** were destroyed because of their blatant sinfulness.

We return to Abram. God's prophet reveals to us the story of how God initiated a covenant with Abram and his descendants:

> *The Lord had said to Abram, "Leave your country, your people and your father's household and go to the land I will show you. I will make you into a great nation and I will bless you; I will make your name great, and you will be a blessing. I will bless those who bless you, and whoever curses you I will curse; and all peoples on earth will be blessed through you." . . .*
>
> *"On that day the Lord made a covenant with Abram, and said, 'To your descendants I give this land,*

from the river of Egypt to the great river, the Euphrates – the land of the Kenites, Kenizzites, Kadmonites, Hittites, Perizzites, Rephaites, Amorites, Canaanites, Girgashites and Jebusites'."

God's prophet reveals to us the story of how God intervened in the natural course of human life, so that Abram and his wife Sarah, far older than normal childbearing ages, could conceive and give birth to a healthy baby, whom they named Isaac:

> When Abram was ninety-nine years old, the Lord appeared to him and said: *"I am God Almighty; walk before me and be blameless. I will confirm my covenant between me and you and greatly increase your numbers. You will be the father of many nations. <u>No longer will you be called **Abram**; your name will be **Abraham**</u>.*

God also said to Abraham:

> *"As for Sarai your wife, you are no longer to call her **Sarai**; her name will be **Sarah**. I will bless her, and will surely give you a son by her. I will bless her so that she will be the mother of nations; kings of peoples will come from her."*

> *Abraham fell face-down; he laughed and said to himself, "Will a son be born to a man a hundred years old? Will Sarah bear a child at the age of ninety?"*

And Abraham, now concerned over the fate of his son **Ishmael** and Ishmael's people, said to God:

74

"If only Ishmael might live under your blessings!"

Then God said, "Yes, but your wife Sarah will bear you a son, and you will call him **Isaac**. I will establish my covenant with him as an everlasting covenant for his descendants after him."

"And, as for **Ishmael**, I have heard you: I will surely bless him; I will make him fruitful, **and will greatly increase his numbers**."

God later continued his covenant through Isaac and Isaac's descendant, **Jacob**. At one encounter, God told Jacob that he was to take the new name "**Israel**."

At another encounter, God assured Jacob of the continuing covenant:

And God said to [Jacob]:

"I am God Almighty; be fruitful and increase in number. A nation and a community of nations will come from you, and kings will come from your body. The land I gave to Abraham and Isaac I also give to you, and I will give this land to your descendants after you."

God also continued his covenant through Joseph, a descendant of Jacob, the man God had renamed "Israel." **Joseph**, while a young man, was sold into slavery by some evil brothers. This occurred about 3,900 years ago. The buyer was a group of traveling foreign merchants, who

75

took him to Egypt, in northeast Africa, and resold him to Potiphar, an official in the Pharaoh's government.

Considering that Joseph was a simple herder of goats and sheep, the resulting exposure to urban, highly organized, and structured **Egypt must have been a powerful educational experience.** Initially prospering as Potiphar's slave, Joseph was given full responsibility for overseeing his owner's house and field servants. But, after some time, Potiphar's wife became vicious toward Joseph, and had him thrown into prison.

But God blessed Joseph while in prison, and permitted him to eventually impress the Pharaoh himself by his ability to correctly interpret dreams. In fact, the superstitious Pharaoh was so impressed with Joseph's predictive power that he told Joseph:

"I hereby put you in charge of the whole land of Egypt."

So, **Joseph** became the Pharaoh's chief administrator. And, it was fortunate for the Israelites that Joseph was in a position to help them, for, about this time a severe famine in their homeland (Canaan) forced all of them to migrate southwestward, along with their herds and flocks, to Egypt, in search of pasture and food. **The famine lasted several years.**

Leaders among the newly arrived Israelites explained their plight before Pharaoh and Joseph:

"Your servants are shepherds, just as our fathers were. We have come to live here awhile, because the famine is severe in Canaan and your servants' flocks have no pasture. So now, please let your servants settle in Goshen."

In response, Pharaoh instructed Joseph:

"Let them live in Goshen. And if you know of any among them with special ability, put them in charge of my own livestock."

Now, with God's help, Joseph had anticipated the famine and, as chief administrator, had arranged for, in previous fruitful years, the storing up of huge grain reserves. Joseph made sure that the newly-arrived Israelites received food, but, in return, they eventually lost possession of the livestock they had brought with them and became enslaved under the Egyptian government, as did the other peoples in the region.

Long after Joseph's death, a new Pharaoh came to power, and became fearful that the now-numerous Israelites might become politically powerful:

"The Israelites have become much too numerous for us. Come, we must deal shrewdly with them, or they will become even more numerous, and, if war breaks out, will join our enemies, fight against us and leave the country."

So, new Pharaoh said:

"Put slave masters over them to oppress them with forced labor, and they built Pithom and Rameses as store cities for Pharaoh. But, the more they were oppressed, the more they multiplied and spread; so the Egyptians came to dread the Israelites and worked them ruthlessly. They made their lives bitter with hard labor in brick and mortar, and with all kinds of work in the fields."

Yet, in spite of this oppression, these simple Israelite herdsmen had learned much from their owners that future generations would use to advantage. And exposure to this learning experience seems to have been the reason that God had permitted His chosen people, for a few generations, to become enslaved in Egypt.

We break away from our story briefly to reflect on a far more familiar slavery experience.

The Israelite experience in Egypt resembled the story of those West Africans who would, much later, be sold into slavery by their fellowmen – their African neighbors – transported across the Atlantic to the Caribbean, North America and South America and resold to farmers in that distant land. These slaves from West Africa, captured by violent nearby tribal warriors, were marched to Africa's Atlantic coastal seaports and sold to captains of slave ships, many of them based in our North East American Colonies. Those slaves from Africa were, too, destined to learn much from their owners – much that future generations would use to advantage.

West Africans fortunate enough to find homes in the American English colonies, especially the expanding Southern Colonies, **numbered 650,000 newly arrived**; they would be sold to work and live as slaves. Many gave birth to and raised children, greatly expanding their numbers.

By the time the Southern States seceded and created the Confederate States of America, the population of slaves living in the USA and the CSA, who had West African appearance to some noticeable degree, totaled **4,000,000**. **The American population of free Africans and their descendants (not slaves but with noticeable West African appearance) totaled 600,000.**

Today, based on the 2020 US census, **46,900,000** people are of significant African ancestry, represented 14.2 percent of our total population.

That original 650,000 number **Expanded Seventy-Two-Fold**, far more than the population expansion in West Africa over the same period of time. And none want to return to West Africa!

They are Americans!

Back to our story, about Moses.

Long after **Joseph's** death, and after several generations of oppression at the hands of Pharaoh's government, God chose a man to lead His people out of bondage. That man was **Moses.** One day, while Moses was tending a flock, God presented Himself from within a burning bush:

> *"I am the God of your father, the God of Abraham, the God of Isaac and the God of Jacob. I have indeed seen the misery of my people in Egypt. I have heard them crying out because of their slave drivers, and I am concerned about their suffering. So, I have come down to rescue them from the land of the Egyptians and to bring them up out of that land into a good and spacious land. . . . I am sending you to Pharaoh to bring my people the Israelites out of Egypt."*

Moses did as God commanded, and presented God's demand to Pharaoh. A contest ensued between God's miraculous signs, as dispensed by **Moses** and his assistant, **Aaron**, and the competing magic tricks dispensed by Pharaoh's court magicians. The miraculous signs became deadly, as God, through the hand of Moses, put the Egyptians through ten plagues: 1, blood; 2, frogs; 3, Gnats; 4, flies; 5, livestock; 6, boils; 7, hail; 8, locusts; 9, darkness, and 10, the firstborn.

After the plague of the firstborn, **the terrified Pharaoh summoned Moses and Aaron and pleaded**:

> *"Up! Leave my people, you and the Israelites! Go, worship the Lord as you have requested. Take your flocks and herds, as you have said, and go. And also bless me."*

This took place about 3,450 years ago.

This became God's fifth covenant, which I shall refer to as, God's "*Covenant of National Presence – Israel.*"

THE ISRAELITES QUICKLY GATHERED TOGETHER and departed Egypt:

> *By day, the Lord went ahead of them in a pillar of cloud to guide them on their way, and, by night, in a pillar of fire to give them light, so that they could travel by day or night.*

Before long, Pharaoh's heart hardened and he dispatched chariots and horsemen to give pursuit. This military force threatened to trap the Israelites against the coast of the **Red Sea**, <u>but God created an immense wind that swept a dry corridor across the seabed, and the</u> **Israelites safely crossed through**.

Soon thereafter, Pharaoh's chariots and horsemen entered the still-open Red Sea seabed corridor in hot pursuit. However, <u>they all drowned when God permitted the wind to stop so the sea would flow back upon them</u>. The Israelites were thereby safely out of Pharaoh's reach.

<u>For about **fifty years**, God led Moses and the Israelites, with their sheep and goats, along a wandering route between Egypt and Canaan, much of it in the desert.</u> During this time, <u>God often appeared through His cloud.</u> <u>A **mobile Tent of Meeting** was constructed according to God's design, so they could worship in God's House wherever they roamed.</u> And the primary religious

treasures were kept in a mobile **"Ark of the Covenant"** for ready transport.

Israeli religious ceremony became highly structured. Numerous laws, inspired by God, structured Israeli society and individual living practices. <u>At one point, God carved upon two stone tablets the laws we call</u> **the "Ten Commandments,"** <u>and directed Moses to present them to the Israelites.</u>

<u>The tablet began with:</u>

> ***"I am the Lord your God, who brought you out of Egypt, out of the land of slavery."***

The Ten Commandments demanded:

1. *"You shall have <u>no other Gods</u> before me...*

2. *"You shall <u>not make for yourself an idol</u>...*

3. *"You shall <u>not misuse the name</u> of the Lord your God...*

4. *"<u>Observe the Sabbath day</u> by keeping it holy...*

5. *"<u>Honor your father and your mother</u>...*

6. *"You <u>shall not murder</u>...*

7. *"You <u>shall not commit adultery</u>...*

8. *"You <u>shall not steal</u>...*

9. *"You <u>shall not give false testimony</u> against your neighbor...*

10. *"You <u>shall not covet</u>..."*

84

After fifty years of purposeful wandering in the desert regions between Egypt and Canaan, God apparently determined that His people were ready to invade the land of Canaan and settle down upon the *"**Promised Land**."*

The wandering phase of their experience was then complete. At this point, Moses had died, his mission concluded. **Joshua had** assumed leadership of the Israeli people. Under Joshua, the Israelites invaded Canaan by first taking the fortified city of Jericho.

Although the walls of Jericho quickly fell with God's help, the fighting to conquer Canaan, and to build a unified nation, was a long process, consuming many generations.

Eventually, a great king, named **Saul**, arose, and Saul's reign marked the start of the final stage of a movement to expand and unify God's chosen people as the nation of Israel. Saul was born about 3,050 years ago.

David succeeded Saul. David led his people in the conquest of the land that would become Jerusalem and much surrounding territory, defeating the Ammonites and the Philistines, and making Israel a prominent nation.

Solomon succeeded David. Solomon oversaw the construction of the first permanent Temple at Jerusalem:

In the four hundred and eightieth year after the Israelites had come out of Egypt, in the fourth year of Solomon's reign over Israel, in the month of Ziv, the *second month, [Solomon] began to build the **temple of the Lord**.*

That was about **2,950 years ago**. But the favored Israelite experience would not last: testing lay ahead.

About 360 years after Solomon built the temple in Jerusalem, **Nebuchadnezzar** led the **Babylonian army** in the conquest of the Israeli people and their capital at Jerusalem. The Babylonians destroyed the Temple, and, by **586 BC**, had carried the more prominent Israeli people back to Babylonia to serve the Babylonian Empire. Eventually, the Persian Empire absorbed the Babylonians, and the Israeli exiles came under the control of **Cyrus, King of Persia**.

Wishing to help the dislocated Israeli people (probably influenced by God), **Cyrus proclaimed**:

"The Lord, the God of Heaven, has given me all the kingdoms of the earth, and He has appointed me to build a temple for Him at Jerusalem in Judah. Anyone of his people among you – may the Lord his God be with him, and let him go up."

And in time, under the leadership of **Ezra** (458 B. C.) and **Nehemiah** (432 B. C.), the Israeli people returned to their homeland and rebuilt Jerusalem and their temple to God.

It seems the Israeli people were **learning to remain a distinct people** capable of surviving the turbulent power shifts that plagued the Middle East. A significant number were not being absorbed into the society of their conquerors, as were other people in the region. God intended that the Israelis not be assimilated, but **survive as a distinct people**, for they were God's messengers to all mankind.

This concludes the history, up to the emergence of the Christian era, as my study has led me to understand it. I hope the telling of this story, which is surely familiar to many, in the above manner, has sharpened your understanding. We move forward now to the present covenant, presented to mankind by **Jesus Christ**.

Chapter 9, God's Sixth Covenant: His New Covenant of Salvation through Faith in Jesus Christ

THE COVENANT BETWEEN GOD AND THE JEWISH PEOPLE came to full flower about 2,000 years ago, (in either 6 or 5 B. C.) with the birth of Jesus Christ, God's Son of Man. [2]

A peak at a map of Europe suggests that Romans, of Italy, were a select segment of Ice Age survivors from north of the Alps mountains.

At the time of the arrival of **Jesus**, the **Roman Empire** was extensive and it included the Israeli people. **Augustus** was Emperor; he was located at Rome. The Empire's existence, its language and/or organization, greatly facilitated communication across far-reaching lands. Perhaps it was for that reason that God chose the era of the Roman Empire to bring his Son to Earth, and there present His *New Covenant* to all mankind.

This covenant between God and all mankind – through His Son, Jesus Christ – is the covenant under which we live today. To the people He encountered, Jesus taught much more than had previously been known about the nature of God and his expectations for man. And, through His disciples, His message, or **Gospel**, was spread

---

[2] (Perhaps God had, on other planets in the Universe, created intelligent beings with souls, but He wisely refrained from revealing that to man.) So, we are concerned only with God's Son for earth, his Son of Man, Jesus Christ, who took on a human body to walk and teach among the Israeli people.

89

throughout the region. Through later generations, His message has been spread throughout the world.

His disciple, **John**, summarized the New Covenant as follows:

"For God so loved the world that He gave His one and only Son, that whoever believes in Him shall not perish, but have eternal life. For God did not send His Son into the world to condemn the world, but to save the world through Him. Whoever believes in Him is not condemned, but whoever does not believe stands condemned already, because he had not believed in the name of God's one and only Son."*

So, God's covenant with the Jewish people was supplemented by His New Covenant with all mankind through **Jesus Christ**.

This was God's sixth covenant, which I have named "His New Covenant of Salvation Through Faith in Jesus Christ."

Today, all people on earth live with the opportunity to benefit from God's Covenant of Salvation Through Faith in Jesus Christ. Yet, subsequent history suggests that a residual covenant must still exist between God and the Jewish people, although the teachings of Jesus would indicate otherwise.

Mary would be the mother of Jesus. She was pledged to Marry Joseph, a descendant of King David, who had led Israel a few centuries earlier. Joseph became alarmed when he realized that his future wife was pregnant. But he decided to pretend that he was the father of the baby growing within Mary after an *"angle of the Lord appeared to him in a dream and said:"*

> *"Joseph, son of David, do not be afraid to take Mary home as your wife, because what is conceived in her is from the Holy Spirit. She will give birth to a son, and you are to give him the name Jesus, because he will save his people from their sins."*

When Mary was close to giving birth, she and Joseph travelled to Bethlehem to pay taxes. Well, it was there, in a stable in Bethlehem, that Jesus was born. Magi from the east saw a blazing star and followed it to Jerusalem, there asking:

> *"Where is the one who has been born king of the Jews? We saw his star in the east and have come to worship him."*

They were told:

> *"Bethlehem in Judah"* because *"the prophet has written: "Bethlehem in the land of Judah . . . for out of you will come a ruler who will be the shepherd of my people Israel."*

But Herod, the Roman King over the Jewish region, having learned of the Magi's visit to Jerusalem, held a meeting with them and asked:

"Go and make a careful search for the child. As soon as you find him, report to me, so I too may go and worship him."

The Magi continued to follow the star until they found baby Jesus with Mary and Joseph in Bethlehem. They worshiped the child, gave him gifts and then left for the west without informing Herod of where Jesus was found.

But Herod was frightened about anyone challenging his authority over Israel, so he ordered his men to kill all boys near Bethlehem 2 years old or younger.

However, Jesus was safe because an angel of the Lord had appeared to Joseph in a dream commanding:

"Get up. Take the child and his mother and escape to Egypt. Stay there until I tell you, for Herod is going to search for the Child and kill him. So, he got up, took the child and his mother during the night and left for Egypt where he stayed until the death of Herod."

"After Herod died, an angel of the Lord appeared in a dream to Joseph in Egypt and said:"

"Get up, take the child and his mother and go to the land of Israel, for those who were trying to take the child's life are dead."

Joseph, Mary and the boy, Jesus, settled in Nazareth, in the district of Galilee, a region in Israel.

In time, Jesus grew to become a man. At this time, John the Baptist, the most important prophet of the era, was preaching in the Desert of Judea and baptizing repentant Jews in the River Jordan. Hearing of this, Jesus, now near 30 years old, walked to the River Jordan and met with John, seeking to be baptized as well.

"But John tried to deter him, saying:"

> *"I need to be baptized by you, and do you come to me?"*

"Jesus replied:"

> *"Let it be so now; it is proper for us to do this to fulfill all righteousness."*

Then John baptized Jesus in the River Jordan.

> *"As soon as Jesus was baptized, he went up out of the water. At that moment heaven was opened, and he saw the spirit of God descending like a dove and lighting on him. And a voice from heaven said:*

> *"This is my Son whom I love; with him I am well pleased."*

After a while, Herod Antipas, who had been designated by Caesar Augustus as ruler over Israel, became fearful of John's gathering followers and threw him in prison at Maechaerus.

From that time on Jesus began to preach:

"Repent, for the kingdom of heaven is near."

At the age of about 30 years, Jesus began teaching the heavenly news of God near the Sea of Galilee. One day he called out to his first four disciples while walking along the shore of the Sea. He called two fishermen brothers, Peter and Simon:

"Come, follow me and I will make your fishers of men. "At once they left their nets and followed him."

"Going on from there, he saw two other brothers, James, son of Zebedee and his brother John. They were in a boat with their father Zebedee, preparing their nets. Jesus called them, and immediately they left the boat and followed him."

Eventually Jesus would accumulate 12 disciples. Thus, Jesus began his teaching of God's desires for men, women and children and how people should deal with evils they encounter.

During his time on Earth, teaching the good news of God, his father, Jesus performed many miracles, including walking on water, using his God-given powers to heal the sick, heal leprosy, heal the demon-possessed, heal paralytics, bring to life a girl who had just died, heal the blind and make the dumb talk, expanding five loaves of bread and two fish to feed five thousand people and expanding seven loaves of bread and a few fish to feed four thousand.

He taught many how to behave as God, his Father, wanted, such as:

Teaching the Beatitudes: "do not murder;" "do not commit adultery;" "love your enemies;" "do not judge, or you too will be judged;" "watch out for false prophets; they come to you in sheep's clothing, but inwardly they are ferocious wolves."

After a year or two, Jesus told his twelve disciples:

"The harvest is plentiful, but the workers are few."

So, at this time, Jesus gathered his twelve disciples, and *"gave them authority to drive out evil spirits and to cure every kind of disease and sickness."* They could now be called apostles!

"These are the names of the twelve apostles:

First, Simon (who is called **Peter**) and his brother **Andrew**; **James, son of Zebedee**, and his brother **John**; **Philip** and **Bartholomew**; **Thomas** and **Matthew** the tax collector; **James, son of Alphaeus** and **Thaddaeus**; **Simon** the Zealot and **Judas** Iscariot."

Jesus instructed the apostles with these words:

"Do not go among the Gentiles or enter any town of the Samaritans. Go rather to the lost sheep of Israel."

After sending out the twelve apostles:

"Jesus went throughout Galilee, teaching in their synagogues, preaching the good news of the kingdom,

95

and healing every disease and sickness among the people."

Eventually, after the disciples were again with him, Jesus decided to make a triumphal entry into the Jewish capital, Jerusalem, which was not far away. When at Bethphage on the Mount of Olives, Jesus sent two disciples ahead, with instructions to borrow a donkey and a colt.

We are now seven days prior to the Crucifixion!

Riding on the donkey while followers laid palm tree leaves on the road before him, Jesus and his disciples, along with many followers, progressed toward Jerusalem. Christians celebrate that day now as "Palm Sunday."

During the first five days, Jesus taught about God along the way, but never spent the night in the city.

Near the end of the fifth day, Jesus gathered his disciples together and told them:

"As you know, the Passover is two days away - and the Son of Man will be handed over to be crucified."

And a bit later, a terrified disciple, **Judas**, decided to secretly betray Jesus in hopes that action would spare his own life.

Since the Passover, is the seven-day Jewish holiday of the Feast of Unleavened Bread, the twelve disciples and Jesus arranged a celebratory supper at a cooperative person's house.

"While they were eating, Jesus took bread, gave thanks and broke it, and gave it to his disciples, saying:

"Take and eat; this is my body."

"Then he took the cup, gave thanks and offered it to them, saying:

'Drink from it, all of you. This is my blood of the covenant, which is poured out for many for the forgiveness of sins. I tell you I will not drink of this fruit of the vine from now on until that day when I drink it anew with you in my father's kingdom.'"

At this gathering Jesus said:

"I tell you the truth, one of you will betray me."

But Judas denied that he would betray Jesus.

After the Last Supper, Jesus and his disciples went out to the Mount of Olives; then as night fell, to Gethsemane.

At dawn, Judas led *"a large crowd armed with swords and clubs, sent from the chief priests and the elders of the people,"* these being the Jewish leaders.

Judas had told the armed crowd:

"The one I kiss is the man; arrest him."

Seeing the kissed man, the armed crowd *"seized Jesus and arrested him."* They *"took him to Caiaphas, the high priest, where the teachers of the law and the elders had assembled."*

In fact, Jesus was being tried before the Sanhedrin, the ancient Jewish court system.

The high priest said to Jesus:

'Tell us if you are the Christ, the Son of God."

"Yes, it is as you say," Jesus replied, "But I say to all of you: In the future you will see the Son of Man sitting at the right hand of the Mighty One and coming on the clouds of heaven."

Then the high priest said

"He has spoken blasphemy!

And the Sanhedrin proclaimed:

"He is worthy of death."

Early in the morning, all the chief priests and the elders of the people bound Jesus and handed him over to Pilate, the Rome-appointed governor.

Before Pilate, Jesus remained silent, replying to none of the charges against him "to the great amazement of the governor."

Well, it was the governor's practice to release a prisoner on the Feast of the Passover as requested by the people. Furthermore:

"At the time they had a prisoner, called Barabas."

"But the chief priests and the elders persuaded the crowd to ask for Barabbas and to have Jesus executed."

Before the manipulated crowd, Pilate asked:

"Which of the two do you want me to release to you?

"Barabas," they answered.

Pilate then asked the crowd:

"What shall I do, then, with Jesus who is called Christ?"

The crowd replied:

"Crucify him!"

And Roman soldiers did just that. They forced Jesus to climb up to Golgotha hill, nailed him to a wooden cross and stood it up in a hole in the ground. There he died. But that is not all.

"At that moment the curtain of the temple was torn in two from top to bottom. The Earth shook and the rocks split. The tombs broke open and the bodies of many holy people who had died were raised to life."

"As evening approached, there came a rich man from Arimathea, named Joseph, who himself had become a disciple of Jesus. Going to Pilate, he asked for Jesus' body, and Pilate ordered that it be given to him. Joseph took the body, wrapped it in a clean linen cloth, and placed it in his own new tomb that he had cut out of the rock. He rolled a big stone in front of the entrance of the tomb and went away. Mary Magdalene and the other Mary (the mother of James and Joseph) were sitting there across from the tomb."

To prevent anyone from stealing the body of Jesus and claiming that he had risen from the dead, Pilate stationed guards at the tomb full time. But those guards would not prevent the resurrection!

"After the Sabbath, at dawn on the first day of the week, Mary Magdalene and the other Mary went to look at the tomb."

At that time:

"There was a violent earthquake. For an angel of the Lord came down from heaven and, going to the tomb, rolled back the stone and sat on it."

"The angel said to the women, 'Do not be afraid. For I know that you are looking for Jesus, who was crucified. He is not here. He has risen, just as he said'."

"Come see the place where he lay. Then go quickly and tell his disciples: 'He has risen from the dead and is going ahead of you into Galilee. There you will see him. Now I have told you'."

"Then the eleven disciples went to Galilee, to the mountain where Jesus had told them to go. When they saw him, they worshiped him; but some doubted. Then Jesus came to them and said, 'All authority in Heaven and on earth has been given to me. Therefore, go and make disciples of all nations, baptizing them in the name of the Father and of the Son and of the Holy Spirit, and teaching them to obey everything I have

commanded you. And surely, I will be with you always,
to the very end of the age.'"

I hope this abbreviated story of Jesus on earth has been helpful. I have used the book of Matthew to present this history.

Chapter 10, The Early Christian Era, the Roman Catholic Church and it's Eastern and Western Branches.

The original Christian Church was the **Roman Catholic Church**, and it split into an eastern (Orthodox) and a western branch.

The western branch of the Roman Catholic Church built elaborate, extensively decorated stone cathedrals throughout Europe, elevated Mary to a companion god, and interposed its priests between God and man.

But by **476 AD** the Roman Empire was overrun by people from the north and northeast. A period referred to as the "Dark Ages" began.

Although no lay Europeans spoke Latin in everyday life, the Roman Catholic Church continued to present its teaching and rituals in the **old Latin language**. Close ties between the Roman Catholic Church and European governments overseen by Kings ensured both stayed in power, and received ample revenue from the people.

We now move forward to the **Reformation, which corresponded closely in time with the European discovery of America**.

The invention of the printing press, and the preaching of Protestant activists, such as **Martin Luther** (German, 1483-1546), **John Knox** (Scotsman, 1514-1572) and **John Calvin** (Frenchman, 1509-1564), ushered in movements throughout the British Isles and Europe aimed at placing

translated Bibles in the hands of the people. Europeans of modest education were able to read *The Bible* in their native language and acquire a personal relationship with God – without the services of a priest. *The Bible's* newly understandable Gospel revealed to European, British Isles and Irish readers a clear image of God and Jesus.

Now enlightened, many criticized the official teachings of the Roman Catholic Church, because they realized that *The Bible* **did not validate the deity of Mary**, and **did not authorize priests** to act as intermediaries between man and God.

Many left the Roman Catholic Church and **formed Protestant churches**, dedicated to the basic teachings of Jesus, as revealed in *The Bible*. Instead of priests, these new Protestant churches had **pastors** and part-time **lay leaders**. Similar churches within a region were often loosely organized, but **they had no "Pope."** Very few Protestant churches had ties with national governments, one notable exception being the Church of England.

By the time British, Scottish, Irish and Northern Europeans began to settle the **New World**, Christianity was the only significant religion in their homeland.

But, a politically powerful religion was in control of vast lands to the south of Europe, including the Middle East. Our story would be incomplete without a discussion of **Islam**. To do that, we go back 900 years, to the year **570**.

Chapter 11, The Rise and Expansion of Political Islam

ISLAM IS THE CREATION OF AN ARABIAN man named **Muhammad**. According to tradition, Muhammad was **born in Mecca** (presently in Saudi Arabia) around the year 570 AD.

At around the age of 40 years, at around the year **610 AD**, Muhammad claimed to be receiving supernatural messages from the angel Gabriel (an angle mentioned in the *Bible*) and he wrote down those alleged messages in a book called the *Koran*.

Muhammad submitted that there was **only one god**, that **Jesus was not the son of that god**, and that Jesus was only a notable prophet.

Muhammad gained around 150 followers in Mecca. Eventually armed conflict broke out between followers of Muhammad, Jewish tribes and Meccans.

Clearly, Muhammad was leading a militant movement bent on conquest and political domination.

By 629, Muhammad had secured political and religious control over Mecca and from there he promulgated Islamic law.

By the time of **Muhammad's death in 632**, an Islamic State, known as the **Rashidun Caliphate**, was established and the area it controlled was growing.

Four subsequent leaders ruled over this Caliphate, considered a **Sunni Islam Caliphate**. By 661, in addition to the vast Arabian Peninsula, the Sunni Islamic State covered **Persia, Syria, Levant, Egypt** and **Eastern North Africa**.

Today, the Islamic world is mostly divided between two different factions, which had historically been in conflict, and remain in conflict today. This schism in Islam began after Muhammad's death in 632.

The faction called **Sunni**, argued that the rightful successor to rule over Islamic states was Abu Bakr, the father of Muhammad's wife Aisha.

The faction called **Shia** argued that the rightful successor was Muhammad's cousin and son-in-law Ail Ibn Abi Talib.

Early on, the Sunni's gained the upper hand, but over the centuries through to today, the Shia have still often sought power.

Today, Muslims considered to be Sunni make up 85 to 90 percent of the world's Islamic population, and those considered Shia make up 10 to 15 percent.

Among Muslims, Sunni are predominant in Indonesia, Southeast Asia, China, South Asia, Africa and most Arab countries.

In contrast, Shia predominate in Iran, Iraq, Lebanon, and are significant in Pakistan, India, Syria and Yemen.

Recent military conflicts between Sunni and Shia include the 8-year **Iran-Iraq War** of 1980-1988 (Shia Iranian Islamic State versus Iraq, primarily a Shia population, but ruled by a Sunni-led government), and the **Syrian Civil War** (a Shia dominated government controlling a rebellious, predominately Sunni population).

Muslim religious leaders mandate that Muslim women cover their bodies to some degree when out among the public. Where Muslims are in the minority, a head scarf suffices. Where insistence on conformity to religious practices predominates, more extensive covering is demanded, even to totally hiding the body in a black sheet of fabric with space for the hands to emerge and for the woman's eyes to see out through two small slits. The rights of Muslim women are severely restricted in countries where Islamists hold control over law, such as in Iran.

Christians view Islam from the outside. We are what Muslims call unbelievers or infidels (**kafirs**), and Muslim rules governing how we are to be treated – rules controlled by Islamic leaders – appear two-faced to us, and can be difficult for us to understand.

Christians believe that the Lord, as revealed by His Son, Jesus Christ, is the only true God. For this reason, only the political aspects of Islam concern Christians. **Dr. Bill Warner** is a widely read expert on Political Islam. He is an American and is not a Muslim. He answers the fundamental question, <u>"What is Islam?"</u> <u>Dr. Warner</u> <u>explains it this way:</u>

"Islam is a cultural, religious and political system. Only the political system is of interest to kafirs (unbelievers) since it determines how we are defined and treated. The Islamic political system is based on the Trilogy (three books) – **Koran** (what Mohammed claimed the angel Gabriel told him), **Sira** (Mohammed's biography) and **Hadith** (Mohammad's traditions). Well over half of Islamic doctrine is political, not religious. **Islam is a political ideology.**"

We now return to early Islamic history.

Following the death of Mohammed, Khalid ibn al-Walid (died in 642) began the next phase of Sunni Islamic conquests. During al-Walid's rule, the Sunni Islamic State reached from the Indus Valley in present day India, across the Middle East, across North Africa, and north into the Iberian Peninsula in present day Spain.

The list of Islamic battles for conquest is very long and bloody. Concerning top Islamic political leaders, their fate is often assassination at the hands of opposition Islamic political forces seeking their turn at the top.

<u>When Islamists are in the minority and are unable to</u> <u>exert control over a country and its people (such as in the</u> <u>United States), leaders pretend to be tolerant of</u> <u>unbelievers, whom they call "**kafirs**."</u>

But when leaders see a chance to dominate a country (establish a controlling Islamic State), <u>they are prone to encourage war</u> and to proclaim a state of "**jihad**", which encourages a war of conquest. Islamic warriors killed in such battles think that they will get ready access to "paradise." That is, the alleged afterlife of Muslim warriors killed in battles in the name of **Allah**, their name for their god. Under such conditions, Islamists are encouraged to **kill kafirs in Allah's name**.

The **Koran** instructs them thusly:

"**Kafirs are the lowest and worst form of life. kafirs can be robbed, murdered, tortured, enslaved, crucified and more.**"

Our story of Islamic history continues.

Using gunpowder technology acquired from China, the Muslim-controlled **Ottoman Empire** came to power during the **early 1300's**. In 1331 Ottomans captured the former Byzantine Christian capital of Nicaea. <u>In 1453 Ottomans captured the Byzantine capital of **Constantinople**</u>, renamed the great city, "**Istanbul**," <u>stripped away all Christian religious symbols from the magnificent **Hagia Sophia cathedral**</u>, dating back to 537 AD, and implemented Islamic law.

<u>I have walked through the stripped Hagia Sophia – a sad sight to behold. The Eastern Roman Catholic Church never recovered.</u>

The Ottoman Empire allied with Germany during World War I and suffered military defeat as well.

Victorious allies broke up the Ottoman Empire and greatly changed the Islamic political map in the Middle East and beyond.

But the Middle East had, and has, **vast oil reserves**. So, money from oil exports has enabled a Muslim resurgence of their passion to empower controlling Islamic States in countries such as Iran, Afghanistan, Iraq and Syria.

Prior to this chapter on Political Islam we were following The Early Christian Era, the Roman Catholic Church and it's Eastern and Western Branches.

Our story of Islam is now complete.

So, we return to Christianity and begin the story of the **New World**.

Chapter 12, God's Sixth Covenant, His New Covenant, Arrives in the New World

THIS IS THE STORY OF HOW GOD'S Sixth Covenant (Salvation through Faith in Jesus Christ) arrived in the Caribbean, North America, Central America and South America.

Europeans discovered the Caribbean Islands and the American continents beginning in **1492**. <u>The **Spanish** arrived first, bringing their Catholic religion and priests</u>.

English settlement of North America began 115 years later at Jamestown, Virginia Colony in 1607, bringing the mainstream English Protestant religion.

<u>Jamestown was thriving by the time **Puritan Separatists** arrived at Massachusetts Bay in 1620</u> to begin the founding of a Puritan-based colony east of the Dutch colony of New Netherland, which had been founded in 1614. New Netherland would become New York and the area settled by Puritan Separatists would become **New England**.

Roman Catholics, of the dominant religion in Spanish and Portuguese-settled Central and South America, were a small minority in the settlement of North America.

<u>In **North America**, several Protestant churches rose to prominence.</u> The **Baptist, Methodist, Presbyterian, Episcopal** and **Lutheran** Churches were the <u>most</u>

111

important in Colonial America, especially in the **Southern Colonies** and subsequent states.

The Society of Friends was important in Pennsylvania.

Additional understanding of the religious issues in what would become New England is worthy of mention:

Soon after the settlement of what would become known as New England, the **Puritan Faction** of the Church of England became increasingly important back home in the British Isles, but created political enemies there by striving to "purify" the souls of non-members through political action. Their effort to secure political control of Parliament eventually failed. Discouraged by that rejection, many Puritans, called **Puritan Separatists**, left England for Massachusetts, and played a major role in further settling what would become known as **New England**.

The **Unitarian** church later arose among the Puritans, but its membership did not fully embrace the teachings of Jesus Christ.

A faction within the Unitarian Church, called **Transcendentalists**, adopted a creative approach to finding God and establishing so-called moral truths.

By the way, their mix of non-Christian religious beliefs permeated New England literary circles, and, between 1830 and 1875, played a major role in establishing a northern States culture of righteous indignation toward Southern States people, which escalated into Southern States Secession, followed by the **Northern States Republican Party's conquest of those legally seceded States**.

Southern States people, both those of European ancestry and those of **African ancestry**, mostly embraced the religious beliefs expressed by Baptists, Methodists, Episcopalians and Presbyterians. They had little to do with Unitarians or Transcendentalists.

Yet, there is much more to the story of Christianity in the New World.

The rest of the story follows.

Chapter 13, Africans Experience God's New Covenant in the New World.

IN A PREVIOUS CHAPTER, you read about God's Sixth Covenant (Salvation through Faith in Jesus Christ) arriving in the Caribbean, Central America, North America and South America. Of course, there is more to this story because:

It was in the New World that Africans by the millions came to know Jesus and accept Him as their savior.

Early in the presentation of *A Christian History of God's Humans from Adam to Today*, I wrote about the migration of a faction of humankind from Africa northward to populate Europe and Asia and of the horrific hardships they suffered during the **Great Ice Age**.

This was the first "Out of Africa" experience for mankind.

And I wrote of the faction of mankind that stayed behind in the African homeland and, as luck would have it, avoided the challenges of surviving harsh Ice Age weather.

We now arrive at a time when the Africans and the Europeans are brought together in large numbers in the Caribbean Islands, North America, Central America and South America.

It began when some Africans were captured by other African tribes near their homelands, taken to the Atlantic coast and sold to ship captains who then took them west across the Atlantic Ocean. Arriving as slaves, they were sold by ships captains to European settlers.

Today, the descendants of these millions of imported African slaves are independent people of a mix of racial inheritance that ranges from pure African to slightly African, living throughout the New World.

The record of this **second great "Out of Africa" experience** needs to also be understood.

Let us look at the numbers.

First, let us ask ourselves a very important question:

During the colonial days of the Caribbean Islands, South America, Central America and North America, **how many people from sub-Sahara Africa were enslaved by neighboring tribesmen, sold to ships captains and shipped across the Atlantic Ocean**?

I will give you the best available answer to that question. But first, remember that it was Africans, of neighboring tribes, that captured and enslaved individuals. Europeans did not have to go inland from the South Atlantic Ocean to do the capturing. The captors just bought their victims to various seaports along the coast of Africa to be sold to ship captains.

The supply of captives must have overwhelmed the carrying capacity of the merchant sailing ships, because it is estimated that **23,500,000 Africans were enslaved** by fellow Africans, but **only 13,400,000 were sold to ship captains** at the West Africa seaports. The difference, 10,100,000, were, for the most part killed or died of disease or malnutrition.

It is estimated that **12,000,000 survived the Atlantic crossing** and **11,300,000 were successfully sold to owners in the New World**. Of the number sold, 7,000,000 are believed to have survived 3 or 4 more years. I have no survival figures beyond the 4-year span.

Now, let us look at how many of those 23,500,000 enslaved Africans were sold to owners in the English colonies of North America.

The best estimate is **575,000** sold through the legal cutoff date of 1808, plus another **25,000 smuggled in** and sold after that.

So, only one in forty enslaved Africans were lucky enough to be sold in the English colonies.

How does this African experience compare to Native Americans?

Well, we know that far fewer Native Americans are living today than were living in North America at the time of Columbus. **Disease and war almost totally destroyed that vast Native population.**

What about those 600,000 Africans who were sold into the English colonies of North America and the states that followed?

Has the population of Americans of African descent grown over time or diminished over time?

Well, America's African-descent population has grown by leaps and bounds!

The 2020 United States Census Bureau reported an estimated **population of 46,779,000 Americans** of pure or partial African ancestry living in America. That is a population that is **78 times the number imported as slaves.**

That is approaching twice the estimated number of all the Africans enslaved by their fellow men in Africa during the era of the Atlantic slave trade. It is more than three times the number of Africans loaded onto ships at West African seaports for transportation to all destinations in the Caribbean, Central America, South America and North America.

I find it helpful to consider these numbers when confronting sensitivities to racial issues in today's world.

Perhaps you will refer to them on occasion as well.

Now, let's fast-forward in time, and explore what life is like in sub-Sahara Africa today.

Mostly gone are the economic and governance benefits that had been given to that vast continent during its colonial era, through generations of hands-on involvement from the many, many Europeans who had come to settle there, raise families there, and contribute, to each African colonial nation, important benefits in many fields, including agriculture, manufacturing, finance, and the workings of a civil society.

But, the departure from Africa, over recent decades, of so many residents of European ancestry and the rapidly growing native African population, has made life in Africa today noticeably more difficult for native Africans. For example, **Elon Musk** left the country of his birth, South Africa, to pursue a college degree in Canada and then America. Subsequently, Elon created two amazing pioneering corporations: Tesla and SpaceX.

I cite **Uganda** and the genocide between the **Hutu** and the **Tutsi**. I cite the economic distress, ethnic terrorism, and criminal lawlessness that have been so prevalent across the continent. I also cite Muslim-led wars to gain political domination. Even the showcase nation of South Africa is hurting. I cite the destructive nature of disease and malnutrition.

I remind you that **Haiti**, although not far from Florida, is essentially a nation populated solely by people from sub-Sahara Africa, and, one would suppose, for similar reasons also suffering. As I write, Haiti is receding into criminal behavior and even cannibalism.

So, why do the natives of sub-Sahara Africa suffer without close association, within their societies, with residents of European ancestry?

The answer seems to me to be straightforward. The answer is quite evident in a simple reading of history. Here is the answer:

"A society made up solely of the native African race will perpetually suffer because it lacks population diversity that includes the economic, scientific, commercial and civil leadership that history tells us can only be generated when a significant part of the population is people of the European or Asian races, and where those races are permitted important political rights.

Nations populated solely by Asian people can thrive. Nations populated solely by European people can thrive. Nations populated solely by African people cannot thrive. Nations of mixed races can thrive, if the African race is not overpowering and dominant.

So, let us ask the question:

Why did God permit 23,500,000 Africans to be enslaved by neighboring tribes, most to be sold to ships captains for transport across the Atlantic to the New World?

I gave you a clue in the opening sentence of this chapter. **Evidence supports the conclusion that God permitted the Atlantic slave trade to allow millions to come from Africa to the New World, suffer hardship, learn important skills, raise families, get to know Jesus, greatly expand and**

thereby enable the harvest of souls from among them and future generations.

It seems to me that, when compared to life in Africa and Haiti, **African Americans are fortunate to be living in the United States, in a mixed-race society**.

A comparison between the opportunities available to people of African ancestry living in the United States, versus people of African ancestry living in Africa, is so dramatic that it is hard to describe in words. Today, people of African ancestry who live in the homeland are cursed with ignorance, political genocide, hunger, and devastating disease.

Should we not suppose that God allowed Africans to be brought to the New World as slaves in order to mix the races of man for the benefit of all humankind and His harvest of Souls?

Chapter 14, Characterizing the Nature of God's Humans Today.

We now move on to characterize the nature of God's humans today.

To encourage further thinking about the nature of mankind all across the world, let us now broaden our view and focus on selected characteristics of the races of man. We now step back to the beginning and then move forward once more.

When God created Adam and Eve in East Africa 200,000 years ago, He did not intend for descendants to be identical to their siblings, their parents, their ancestors, or to Adam and Eve. God intended that we humans experience genetic variations like all other life on Earth. God wanted and expected us to become more and more diverse as the centuries went by. Since Adam and Eve, mankind has experienced over 10,000 generations, giving ample opportunity for the expression of important genetic variation among today's people.

I believe God is pleased with the results of the human evolution that has occurred over those 10,000 generations. In that outcome He probably sees both challenges and opportunities. As we ponder those challenges and opportunities we proceed forward

Let us explore a few important characteristics of individuals, families and the human races.

There are differences in people that have been passed down through their racial ancestry. The differences in appearance are perhaps most obvious, but the differences in various abilities are of more importance. So, I need not discuss the appearance differences among the races of man, such as skin color, hair color, etc. I assume all readers are familiar with appearance differences.

So, what I need to do is tell you about three non-appearance characteristics of individuals, and describe how those characteristics are distributed among individuals, and among the races of man. The three characteristics I would like to discuss are: **cognitive ability**, **athletic ability** and **musical ability**.

But first, let me lay a foundation for this discussion by summarizing the basic science of genetic inheritance.

An individual's innate cognitive ability, athletic ability and musical ability seems to result from mixtures of that individual's genetic inheritance and that individual's environmental interactions. The two most important environmental factors are parental care and diet history, from conception through childhood.

But it is important that you understand that environmental factors are less important than genetic factors. Scientific studies, particularly those based on identical twins separated at birth, indicate that genetic inheritance accounts for between 80% and 40% of an individual's innate cognitive ability. I am persuaded to embrace Herrnstein and Murray's approximation of 60%

genetic inheritance of cognitive ability. Furthermore, I am persuaded to attribute about 60% of an individual's athletic ability and musical ability to genetic inheritance, as well.

Siblings in a family vary in cognitive ability, athletic ability and musical ability because, at the time each individual is conceived, he or she consists of a unique combination of genetic instructions, which were synthesized from the **genetic offerings that were derived from four grandparents**. The same genetic mechanism is obviously present when examining differences within, and between, the races of man. If four grandparents of the same race can contribute a genetic mix that results in the span of cognitive ability typically observed among siblings in a single family, then surely it is likely that genetic factors can explain the differences observed between individuals from many families within the same race.

Likewise, genetic factors surely contribute to the differences observed between groups of individuals belonging to different races. Looking at the issue from a different perspective, I am also persuaded that there is no scientific reason to suppose that racial differences are limited to outward appearance factors such a skin and hair color. There is nothing in the workings of genetic reproduction that restricts genetic variations to outward appearance characteristics.

So, with that genetics background preface, we continue.

Now, we know that man began the long process of evolving into the African, European and Asian races about 110,000 years ago, and that time span equates to 5,000 generations. It is further important to recognize that there is no known mechanism in genetics that would ensure, over a span of 5,000 generations, that race A and race B would contain the same genetic mix of cognitive abilities expressed as a mean, an average or a range. This reasoning would also apply to the genetic mix of athletic abilities or musical abilities.

So, surely, it is likely that, for genetic reasons alone, the cognitive ability, athletic ability and musical ability of millions of individuals in race A can, and ought to, differ from the cognitive ability, athletic ability and musical ability of millions of individuals in race B, presented as means, averages and ranges.

And it is apparent that it was God's plan that people would be different – that a few would have exceptional cognitive ability and that some of those would make discoveries that would benefit all of mankind.

You see, over the centuries, it has been a few descendants of those ice age cave dwellers – a few of them, here and there, blessed with amazing inventive and organizational skills – that have contributed tremendous life-changing advances which have so benefitted mankind all over the world.

These men were of the "Out of Africa" races.

They have brought us written languages, printing, global exploration, steam engines and railroads, electricity, great advances in chemistry, biology and agriculture, internal combustion engines, great medical advances, trucks, automobiles, aircraft and space ships, electric vehicles, highly automated and economical manufacturing factories, and on and on the list goes. Without such men (there were a few women, too) mankind would still be dependent on beasts of burden for agriculture, construction and transportation – and feeding today's expanded human population would be impossible.

And, we must remember that an individual, no matter how gifted cognitively, cannot create great technical advances alone. <u>Those advances highlighted in our history have been enabled by the expanding ability of people to communicate among themselves over greater and greater distances, thereby facilitating the accumulation of knowledge essential to the advancement of civilization</u>. Think letters being mailed, printed books, then telecommunications, computers, and now the internet.

So, I suggest you join me in giving thanks to such men and those few women.

And I suggest that God's plan to see mankind suffer through the ice age in caves was to spur human evolution forward to enable men of

exceptional cognitive ability to be born thousands of generations after Adam and Eve.

What about the distribution of athletic ability?

What do we observe regarding athletic ability here in America? Well, it is obvious to any objective observer of American athletic competitions that boys and girls, and men and women, <u>with at least 25 percent African ancestry dominate sports teams where athletic ability is essential to successful competition</u>. The best example is the game of basketball, where athletic quickness and leaping ability are essential to outstanding play. <u>Often, on professional teams, we see that four or even all five players on a team on the basketball court are of African ancestry</u>. African Americans star on football teams, particularly where athletic skill is most important, most notably at wide receiver. African Americans dominate track and field events, especially at short-distance races. By watching the Summer Olympics one can readily see that <u>people of African ancestry are dominant in the core track and field events</u>.

Soon after Africans arrived in America, many of them learned the European's more complex music scale, and began to excel in music.

They sang in harmony. They learned to play European instruments. They composed music. <u>They eventually invented new musical forms, such as **Jazz** and the **Blues**</u>.

128

Today, African American musicians and singers are more prominent in popular music than one would expect, considering their share of the American population.

On balance, it appears that the musical and singing ability of African Americans is at least equal to the musical and singing ability of European Americans and in some ways might be superior.

If you question that, listen to the **Kings Return** men's quartet singing "The Lord's Prayer" a cappella on U-Tube. The quartet consists of Gabe Kunda, Vaughn Faison, J. E. McKissic and Jamall Williams. They are outstanding. They live in Dallas Texas. In fact, my wife and I recently attended their March, 2024 concert in our home town.

<u>So, African Americans hold admirable talent for music and superior talent for athletics. On the other hand, the "Out of Africa" races have, collectively speaking, an advantage in cognitive ability</u>.

We now move to the closing chapter.

There, you can ponder conclusions and consider questions prompted by your reading of *"A Christian History of God's Humans from Adam to Today."*

Chapter 15, Conclusions and Questions for You to Ponder

MY PRESENTATION IS NOW COMPLETE. You now perceive **my** understanding. So, let us together explore some pertinent questions and use them as a way for you to arrive at attaining **your** understanding.

As you review questions numbers 1 through 15, which follow on the next page, reflect on your past understanding and beliefs and the basis upon which you have come to embrace each one.

At the same time, please, allow scientific truths to prevail over so-called "politically correct truths."

Listen to what we have before us, handed down to us in our Bibles, keeping in mind that those words, those revelations by our Lord, were originally selected to match the level of scientific and geographic understanding of the first people to hear them, enabling those first-to-hear to pass said revelations to later generations, who would eventually commit them to writing.

Again, we observe that God was not in the business of teaching science and geography to His people. Hopefully, the exercise below will broaden your mind and enable you to acquire greater meaning from future study of the issues presented herein.

I am now through with the presentation of God's creation of the Universe (big bang); the evolution of galaxies, stars and planets; the evolution of our Earth into a habitable planet; the evolution of life on Earth; God's creation of man (Adam and Eve); the subsequent evolution and life advances of their descendants; the diversification of mankind into races (surviving the Ice Age in caves); God's six covenants designed to give guidance to mankind; migration to the **Americas** (Natives, Europeans and Africa slaves); three important characteristics of mankind (cognitive, athletic and musical abilities), and how they are expressed in man's diversity resulting from the **evolution of 10,000 generations**.

As I close, I invite you to ponder the following questions:

1. Did God create the Heavens and the Earth and, subsequently, its living creatures, using natural forces and evolutionary selection to advantage?

2. Do you agree that man is not just a highly evolved animal; that God, while employing supernatural powers, did select a site in East Africa about 200,000 years ago and there did create man in his own image?

3. Did God thereafter allow man to diversify through evolution, and did He push a portion of mankind out of Africa about 110,000 years ago, and, by 30,000 years ago, had Ice Age hardships diversified man to include the "Out of Africa" races we call European and Asian?

4. Did the European and Asian races, by being forced to overcome Ice Age cold by hunkering down in dark, but warm caves, lose athletic skills, but gain more helpful coping skills? Are much of the differences observed in the cognitive skills and athletic skills of individuals who are alive today rooted in their ancestor's different experiences in cold or temperate climates during the past Ice Age?

5. By sometime between 30,000 and 15,000 years ago, had man eliminated all hominid animals that had preceded his arrival on Earth?

6. Did the Earth's most advanced civilization thrive near and around Black Lake and, about 7,600 years ago, suffer a horrendous flood that scattered survivors, including Noah, away to the North, to the South, to the East and to the West?

7. Did God later establish a covenant with Abraham, whose descendants became the Jewish people? Did He later establish a covenant with Moses, to prepare the Israeli people for nationhood?

8. Did God use the Jewish people as His witnesses, so, through them, He would become known to people from Egypt to Canaan to Persia to Rome, for the purpose of preparing the world for the arrival of His Son?

9. During the days of the Roman Empire, did God make His New Covenant with all mankind through

His Son, Jesus Christ? Did God, through Christ, command His disciples to spread the Gospel throughout the world?

10. Did Jesus Christ teach that "salvation is by faith, not by works, lest any man should boast"?

11. Should a Christian evangelize others by example, and by spreading the Gospel, but not by forcing his or her religious attitudes upon others?

12. Is it possible for any religion to truthfully glorify itself by imposing its religious attitudes and behaviors upon people who are not believers but are forced to conform?

13. If those Europeans that migrated to the New World had not purchased bonded Africans (slaves), would there have been significant westward migration out of Africa during the last 500 years – would there be a significant population of people of African ancestry in the Americas today?

14. Are today's African Americans better off in every respect than their distant cousins who remain in the African homeland – is that why essentially none wish to migrate to Africa?

15. Is America fortunate to have many people of partial or pure African ancestry living among us throughout our nation, thereby making ours a nation of racial diversity and not of one race? My answer to the final question is "yes." I hope yours is as well.

I expect you know how I am answering these questions. What about you?

We are now arriving at the end of my presentation, *A Christian History of God's Humans from Adam to Today.* If you found the last chapter with its emphasis on understanding racial differences an uncomfortable experience, I apologize.

But it is hard to truly present the subject of the evolution, over **10,000 generations**, of God's people, subsequent to **Adam** and **Eve**, without digging into such racial details.

Dr. Martin Luther King emphasized that people should be "judged by the strength of their character, not by the color of their skin." I totally agree.

Keep in mind that you can gain knowledge from my study even when you do not agree with all that I have embraced. Examine it bit by bit, and apply what you find helpful. Why?

Because, this study is irrevocably dedicated to my original objective: in all endeavors seek the truth – *"for the truth shall set you free."*

And I am hopeful that you, too, will become a **Truth-Seeker.**

References to this Study

Note: The translation of the Holy Bible used throughout this study is the *New International Version*, copyrighted in 1978. I find it to be the most accurate translation and the easiest to understand among the translations available today. It is the one I have read from cover to cover. Other references follow.

1. *The Book of Man, The Human Genome Project and the Quest to Discover our Genetic Heritage*, Walter Bodmer and Robin McKie, Oxford University Press, 1994, 1997 paperback. This book and *African Exodus* below, when published, were revolutionary windows into how, for the first time in history, <u>examinations of the human genome was revealing, all around the world, human inheritance and racial ancestry</u>.

2. *African Exodus, The Origins of Modern Humanity*, Christopher Stringer and Robin McKie, Henry Holt and Company, New York, 1996. The note above applies here as well.

3. *National Geographic Magazine*, July 2000, page 108. The sites at Dolni Vestonice and Pavlov are on the Dyje River, a tributary of the Danube, in present-day southern Czech Republic, about 700 miles upstream of what was Black Lake before the great flood. <u>Here is amazing proof of early advanced civilizations upstream from **Black Lake**</u>.

4. *The Southeastern Indians*, Charles Hudson, The U. of Tennessee Press, 1976, paperback reprint, 1994, pages 36 to 42. <u>This explains how European diseases killed off almost all of the **Natives in North America** soon after Europeans arrived</u>.

5. *Noah's Flood, The New Scientific Discoveries about the Event that Changed History*, William Ryan and Walter Pitman, Simon &

Schuster, New York, 1998. Amazing. This discovery, proving and dating the **flooding of Black Lake**, thereby creating **the Black Sea**, is fundamental to understanding the flood story in the Bible

6. *National Geographic Magazine*, April 1999. This gives details on long-ago human civilization at the time Black Lake was flooded by saltwater.

7. *The Charlotte Observer*, February 27, 2005. This reference is a remarkable and in-depth **report on the Atlantic slave trade** by reporters of the *Charlotte Observer* newspaper of Charlotte, NC. It was printed in their February 27, 2005 issue as a contribution to Black History Month. The story is presented as a full page color poster. The information was derived from several important studies of the Atlantic slave trade, with those sources properly noted.

8. *The Bell Curve, Intelligence and Class Structure in American Life*, Richard J. Herrnstein and Charles Murray, The Free Press, New York, 1994. This very important work by Herrnstein and Murray has been so bitterly denounced by so many vocal advocates of political correctness that you ought to suspect that it must be very important. That it is! **It is both very important and also scientifically valid**. I strongly support their work and rely on it. When you observe comments such as, "This study has been discredited," please ignore them and ask, "Show me a better study, likewise full of numbers and measures, that **improves** on the work of Herrnstein and Murray."

9. *Political Islam,* Bill Warner (a series of books are available that gives understanding to Islam and its political objectives). **See www.politicalislam.com**.

A listing of Published Books Authored by Howard Ray White, all available on Amazon as print books, most as e-books, some as audio-books, plus his 80 TV Shows.

Historian Howard Ray White's publication of *A Christian History of God's Humans from Adam to Today* has a long history. The publication history follows:

The story of *A Christian History of God's Humans from Adam to Today* began as a chapter in Volume 2 of *Bloodstains: An Epic History of the Politics that Produced and Sustained the American Civil War and the Political Reconstruction that Followed,* by me, Howard Ray White. Volume 2 of that book series, subtitled *The Demagogues,* was self-published in 2003.

In 2014 the author published his Christian history of God's Humans under the title, *Understanding Creation and Evolution: A Biblical and Scientific Study.*

In 2018, with the encouragement and advice of Dr. Clyde N. Wilson, the author published an updated version of the story through Shotwell Press, Inc. under the title, *Understanding Creation and Evolution,* the author retaining his copyrights to the content.

In 2023, the author, seeking an avenue to increase readership, self-published a slightly revised version under the title, *God's Humans, from Adam to Today.*

In 2024, the author further edited this same history and added lots of punch (underlining sentences and bolding important words), added a chapter on Jesus and republished his book under the title *"A Christian History of God's Humans from Adam to Today."*

Now eighty-six years old, the author has concluded his massive writing effort.

Empowered by his long career as a chemical engineer and as a professional engineer, Howard Ray White, in 2023, self-published *Musk, Ford, Wrights, Amazing Americans who Fundamentally Advanced Human Travel.* Therein, in this first edition, are comparative biographies of Elon Musk, Henry Ford and the Wright Brothers, together in one book. Readers will learn how Musk, through his Tesla company, revolutionized the excitement and popularity of the electric vehicle and, through his SpaceX company, revolutionized space travel, formerly solely government endeavors. In subsequent editions readers will probably learn about his SpaceX company going to the Moon and to Mars.

Other books.

***Bloodstains**, an Epic History of the Politics that Produced and Sustained the American Civil War and the Political Reconstruction that Followed.* A history in four volumes: Vol. 1, *The Nation Builders;* Vol. 2, *The Demagogues;* Vol. 3, *The Bleeding;* Vol 4, *The Struggle for Healing.* This is a vastly detailed reference that should be in your library.

Understanding Abe Lincoln's First Shot Strategy (Inciting Confederates to Fire First at Fort Sumter). This is a fast read, telling well this critical history. Sadly, this critically important history is omitted or misrepresented in schools, colleges and universities.

Understanding "Uncle Tom's Cabin" and "The Battle Hymn of the Republic;" How Novelist Harriet Beecher Stowe and Poet Julia Ward Howe Influenced the Northern Mind. A quick read; important story.

How to Study History when Seeking Truthfulness and Understanding; Lessons Learned from Outside Academia. A brief and compelling guide for all readers of history who seek truth instead of passing an exam at school. Good for parents and grandparents, too. Every teenager should read this!

How Southern Families Made America: *Colonization, Revolution and Expansion from Virginia Colony to the Republic of Texas, 1607 to 1836.* **This is a must read!** Southern families were the Nation Builders. Here is a thorough documentation that tells their history and amazing stories of important Southern leaders, Andrew Jackson and Sam Houston. Is your ancestry Southern? Please get this book and feel the joy within.

The CSA Trilogy, An **Alternate** History/Historical Novel in three volumes about Our Vast and Beautiful Confederate States of America — A Happy Story in Three

Parts of What Might Have Been — 1861 to 2011. I suggest you don a dreamer's cap and enjoy a happy story concluding with celebrating the 150th Anniversary of the large, successful Confederate States of America:

Book 1: *How We Confederates Won Our Independence, 1861 to 1862.*

Book 2: *How We Confederates Invited Cuba, Northern Mexico, Russian America and Hawaii to Join Our Federation of States, 1862 to 1877.*

Book 3: *How We Confederates Preserved Our Values while Developing the World's Greatest Economy, 1878 to 2011.*

<u>Wartime Struggles of a Virginia Slave Family</u>. During Four Years of Civil War Across Virginia, a Slave Family Struggles to Keep Safe and Stay Together as They Ask: "<u>Who Are Our True Friends, White People of the North, or White People of the South?</u>" A Historical Fiction Novel full of true history. Here you live through the war in and near Richmond; you follow my intelligent slave family's struggles; you live through the true history of Edmund Ruffin and his family and the true history of Mrs. Robert E. Lee and her children.

<u>Rebirthing Lincoln</u>, *How an Illinois Lawyer Kept Secret His Illegitimate Birth and Won the 1860 Presidential Nomination of the Northern States Republican Party.* This is the most truthful biography ever written about President Abraham Lincoln. It is highly unlikely that Kentuckian Thomas Lincoln was the biological father of baby Abraham. Instead, the boy's father was likely Abraham Enloe a prominent western North Carolinian. When little Abe was about two years old, his mother, Nancy Hanks of western North Carolina, married Thomas Lincoln and the couple raised little Abraham in Kentucky. How did politically ambitious Abraham Lincoln keep his true-birth secret? That is the underlining story in *Rebirthing Lincoln*, which presents a Lincoln biography from birth to 1) his law career in Illinois, 2) his becoming President, 3) to his refusing to seek peace and, 4) instead, to his launching a war of conquest, which lasted four years and resulted in one million unnecessary American deaths. This is a truthful biography, not an alternate history, not a novel. This is a MUST READ!

Why and How the North Conquered the South. An essential quick read. "Please just devote 3 or 4 hours to reading this concise, yet complete, history so you will know the truth of America's most horrific catastrophe, **a tragedy that resulted in one million unnecessary American deaths.**"

Three books edited by Howard Ray White:

Advancing American Reading Achievement During the Great Depression: a 1939 Comparative Study of Seventh Grade White and African American Children in

Segregated Nashville, Tennessee Schools, by Dr. Larry Jordan Willis, my father-in-law.

Understanding Granddad Through His Poetry, the Poetry of Tennessean John Andrew White (1874-1951), with story and editing by grandson, Howard Ray White. Jr. I dropped the "Jr." after Dad died.

Springfield Girl, a Memoir, by Martha Frances Bell White, with additions by son Howard Ray White. My mother wrote this and I published it. Following her death, I completed her story and created this, the second edition.

One book that my wife, Judith, and I jointly authored:

Remembering While We Still Can, the Memoir of Judith and Howard White's Southern Family. We both wrote this for our 60th wedding anniversary.

One book that my wife, Judith Willis White, wrote about her Hunt family of Easley, South Carolina:

Memories of Easley, South Carolina, My Wonderful Grandparents, Leigh and Camella Hendricks Hunt and Their Descendants, by granddaughter Judith Willis White. This is a wonderful book about Judith's grandparent's family and her visits while growing up.

Two books authored by sixteen members of the Society of Independent Southern Historians, which I co-founded (I was an editor and contributing author here):

Understanding the War Between the States, A Supplemental Booklet by 16 Writers that Enables a More Complete and Truthful Study of American History (Middle School, High School, College and Beyond), by 13 members of the Society of Independent Southern Historians, Howard Ray White, co-editor.

American History for Home Schools, 1607 to 1885, with a Focus on Our Civil War, also written by 13 members of the Society of Independent Southern Historians. This is very similar to the book above.

Howard Ray White's TV Shows

To view any of my 80, 30-minute TV shows, from the weekly Series titled "**True American History**," go to **www.vimeo.com** and query "Howard Ray White" on your computer or query Vimeo on your smart streaming TV.

My Close:

I feel blessed when Americans, who seek the truthful history concerning the horrible American Civil War, turn to my books for enlightenment. It is so easy. Just go to **www.amazon.com** and query "Howard Ray White." A complete list of my books will appear for your review, ranging from the large *Bloodstains* 4-volume set to quick reads such as *Understanding Abe Lincoln's First Shot Strategy.*

And I thank you for reading *A Christian History of God's Humans from Adam to Today.*

Thank you and God bless every one of you.

www.ingramcontent.com/pod-product-compliance
Lightning Source LLC
Chambersburg PA
CBHW061729020426
42331CB00006B/1172